Time to Come Clean

Time to Come Clean

Rescuing Jesus from Christianity

Tom Hall

ISBN: 9781598153347

Contents

Dedication

This book is dedicated to:

Robert Cooper, who asked me to share his pulpit and thus expanded my world;

Robert Funk, who let me edit books for his team of scholars, and thus provided a priceless educational experience;

Lloyd Geering, who in accepting me as wordsmith, collaborator, and friend has provided me with daily intimations of fulfillment and gratitude.

Preface

Were it not for several years of occasional nagging, I would probably not have undertaken this avuncular critique of twenty-first century Christianity. But my dear wife and convivial daughter-in-law eventually tired of my grumblings about the lack of religious knowledge and understanding that seems to afflict both the pulpit and the pews—and likely tired even more of my lengthy corrective dissertations. "You ought to write a book," they said.

I refused, of course, for talking is much easier than writing. But over the years it had become clear to me that many people who should know better simply assume the Hebrew and Christian scriptures to have been arranged in the chronological order of their composition, and worse yet evince little awareness of their many errors and self-contradictions. I grew frustrated. The problem was exacerbated when some three years ago I watched President Bush's funeral on television. One of his sons expressed the assurance that the family would one day be reunited in Heaven, and the officiating clergyman, who had witnessed Bush's final moments, observed that "he left this life for the next" and would soon be "in the loving arms of Barbara and Robin." Here were two cultured, well educated, and highly respected leaders passing out theological taffy that I can only hope they didn't really believe. The tipping-point was when I heard one too many iterations of "Well, I suppose you're right about that, but I could never say such a thing in church!" When you can't tell the truth about religious matters in church, things have come to a pretty pass. So I started scribbling.

I have tried to write for the general reader and employ a bare minimum of academic trappings, but after years of editing scholarly texts, I may have grown a bit too formal. For this and a less than strict commitment to careful organization I apologize. I also beg forgiveness for views that may at times seem harsh, but having more than once been thanked for avoiding an ephectic position, I am at times blunt.

Besides, we are in trouble. Our suicidal attacks on the ecosystem that supports us are becoming indisputable and an undisciplined response to COVID-19 has killed more than half a million Americans; yet every night crowds flock into huge stadiums aglow with light produced by fossil fuels to watch people play games. And recently we learned that church membership has fallen below fifty percent for the first time in history. Yet we need more than ever the social cohesion and commitment to ethical norms and responsible lifestyles that churches have long provided. Why the defections; why are so many joining what the late Episcopal Bishop John Shelby Spong called the Church Alumni Association?[1]

I submit that it is largely because for many of us the perceived world has changed: we no longer live in the three-story world of the past, and have outgrown literal belief in myths, magic, miracles, and other forms of supernaturalism. We live in a vast cosmos that has no above and below, but is a unitary phenomenon governed by universal laws and principles not subject to the whims of imagined entities. Centuries of science and critical thinking have made secular humanists of us, and we will no longer agree to govern our lives in accordance with fairy-tales ancient or modern. Like Sgt. Friday we want "just the facts."

Unfortunately, we have a dangerous habit of ignoring certain facts—like climate change and the need for personal responsibility. And this is the sort of bad habit that a responsible religious tradition might persuade us to recognize and strive to overcome. Our churches could do much to help us find a path to salvation. But it will have to be a new path. The old dream of salvation is a chimera. It's time to come clean.

And now it is time for gratitude. First in line are the many Westar scholars I have had the honor and privilege to know and work with and learn from; they have enabled me to enjoy a fascinating and fulfilling retirement career I never dreamed of. Next, my thanks go out to Barbara and Katy, the two wonderful women whose badgering I have noted above and whose continuing support I now acknowledge. Above all I am indebted to my daughter, Elly Hall, whose intellectual independence and acuity have cheered me on,[2] and without whose patience, computer skills, and careful editing I could not have brought this eruption to what I hope will prove a successful conclusion.

Tom Hall—Foster, RI. October 2021

---

1. Note the comment of a former student (Ponaganset High School, Class of '62) to whom I sent copies of Spong's recent obituary and his now famous "Twelve Theses":

   "Man, I really like this guy! He has addressed all the things that made me fall away from the church . . . He's like a prospector gleaning bright nuggets to share with us."

2. "Some years ago the speaker at a church-sponsored discussion on 'Intercessory Prayer' highlighted two case studies in which babies in a Neonatal Intensive Care Unit, for whom a group of nuns prayed, had measurably better outcomes than a similar group who were not prayed for. When I asked whether this "evidence" suggested that God's grace is for sale, the speaker summarily ended the discussion.

   The following Sunday our pastor kindly informed me that my comments had led him to rethink his beliefs on the role and efficacy of prayer. " E.H.

Apologia

The church's refusal to see the historical dimensions of its life
can be seen in the often-used description of the church as
"divinely instituted." This is tantamount to special pleading, an
avoidance of the fact that this or that structure is an historical
development resulting from the decisions of human beings.
—Arthur Dewey, "Ecclesial Tectonics," §7.12

A couple of years ago I found myself sitting next to a long-time friend at the banquet that closed the Spring meeting of the Westar Institute.[3] I hadn't seen him for two or three years, but knew he had recently retired from forty years as a UCC minister, the last twelve as pastor of a large and thriving church in southern California. After a few old-friend pleasantries, I asked him where he currently attended church. I did not ask as one seeking a particular place of worship to attend, but simply as one who had of late been unable to find a church whose spiritual aspirations were not stultified by antique beliefs and practices. Alas, I learned that he too had pretty much given up attending church because he could not find a congregation that was sufficiently progressive in its theology and social outreach to suit one whose pastoral mantras had long challenged his flock to think as adults:

Think for yourself; your minister could be wrong,
What you believe is less important than how you behave, and
We are concerned with Jesus' message, not his divinity.

And since he lives in a large city and I in a small rural town, I was not encouraged.

Nor has further experience provided reason for much optimism. Apparently most mainline ministers are afraid to deviate from outmoded creeds and liturgies lest they ruffle a single theological feather and thus lose a contributor to the weekly offering. Worse yet, they seem unwilling to undertake any critical examination of scripture, and therefore misconstrue and even falsify the very Bible that some of them describe as inerrant and infallible. In doing so, of course, they are

---

3. The Westar Institute, co-founded in 1985 by Robert W. Funk and John Dominic Crossan, is comprised of about a hundred Fellows, all of whom are highly qualified New Testament scholars, and some 1600 Associate Members, who are interested non-specialists.

1

obliged to overlook or conceal its many self-contradictions, historical errors, theological inconsistencies, forgeries, and obviously false claims.

The result is that two former Christian pastors—one an authentic church leader and one an uncredentialed but well-read and experienced amateur—are hard-pressed to find places of worship that not only permit but actively encourage intellectual honesty in both pew and pulpit. What a fine kettle of fish! A sad commentary, methinks, on the present state of a 2000–year-old tradition. Can anything be done to save it from itself—to call back some who have left in disgust or despair, and to attract others who seek a more spiritual life?

The admittedly presumptuous aim of this essay is to offer a number of proposals that might be effective in such an undertaking. To be sure, they will not all have a universal appeal, but since no two of us have identical beliefs or spiritual inclinations, a number of them might prove of value in saving a noble religious quest from gradual decline into a salvation cult that mocks the genius of its founder's vision and proclamation.

Such a bumptious statement of purpose demands a confession that reflects both meanings of that word: a declaration and an admission. First off, my declaration: I was raised in a small Rhode Island town and more or less regularly attended the local Baptist church where my mother, the daughter of a once prominent New Jersey minister, was an active member. I cannot say that any of that had a strong influence on my thinking, but neither did it tend to make religion distasteful. In fact, when I went away to college I showed up fairly regularly at the local Congregational church because the minister's sermons made me think and the Friday night square dances he led in the church basement were an enjoyable part of my life. Coincidentally, the Dartmouth Christian Union sponsored The Hanover Hoedowners, a group of square-dance musicians I led for three years, and its faculty advisor, the irrepressible Rev. George Kalbfleisch, talked me into taking an occasional turn at leading the college's daily fifteen-minute chapel service. I had never been a doctrinaire believer, and under his tutelage I began to question a number of conservative notions. A key awakening came from Professor Philip Wheelwright's little pamphlet "Philosophy of the Threshold," which made the crucial point that Heaven and Hell are not place names but symbols, and thereby cast the entire Christian narrative of salvation history into serious question. Thus, it was that in my junior year I began to doubt the wisdom of aiming for the pulpit, a path that would likely involve imposing a good deal of religious skepticism on a typical congregation pretty well set in their traditional beliefs. Accordingly, I signed up for a few courses in the education department and aimed for the classroom instead. And thereafter I was sufficiently busy with a year of graduate school, six in the Navy, and five as an English teacher that I gave little thought to matters theological.

But when I bought a home in Foster in 1966, I decided to see whether the local Baptist Church might have anything to offer. It did, for the Rev. Robert C. Cooper was one who followed the example of the nominal founder of the faith: he was not a preacher, but a teacher. As a fellow expositor of a not dissimilar subject, I was won over immediately, especially since he often reminded us that incredible assertions need not be believed. Bob was a member *in pectore* of Westar's Jesus Seminar twenty years before it was founded. I followed him when he took a pulpit in nearby Connecticut, and when a year or so later he asked me to take his place the following week so that he could fill in for an old friend, I protested that I was not up to the challenge. But it turned out that I was; and soon I was filling in occasionally, then regularly, and at last took over preaching duties at his two churches for several years. One eventually closed down when all but a few members died, and I left the second to avoid a potential schism over my desire to remove trinitarian language from the Doxology and Gloria Patri. This was a mildly amusing irony, since I had long since written the "body and blood" passages out of the communion service without any objections!

Some months thereafter I discovered a Universalist congregation that had been unable to support a minister and was glad to try out a lay preacher who would serve without pay. That stint went very well for three or four years—with a revised Lord's Prayer, communion service, and two Unitarian liturgies—and even saw a temporary increase in attendance. But at last enough people dropped out or moved away that it seemed I was not helping the cause, so I expressed my regrets and left. Then I hit a streak of luck: a nearby pastoral Quaker meeting could no longer afford their paid minister, and was willing to try a relatively new but very affordable member in the pulpit. The non-liturgical service and the general makeup of the congregation proved a good fit for about three years, but over a period of eight or nine months a recently joined young family moved west and three other staunch supporters of my pedagogical homiletics died. Then, on returning from a speaking engagement at a New Zealand Sea of Faith conference, I was unceremoniously sacked. Midwestern Quakers, it seems, tend to be rather doctrinaire, and one such parishioner was outraged that I had distinguished between the man Jesus and the mythic personage later accorded the honorific title "The Christ."

But even an ill wind blows some good, for now I had more time to read and study. Besides, I had enjoyed many years of learning and sharing what I learned with people for whom the Christian tradition had substance and meaning. And I had early on found in Westar not only a source of information vital for any serious minister, but also a group of scholars who were glad to have on board a former English teacher who had a helpful knowledge of scripture, a considerable skill in polishing prose, and a wish for nothing more than a word of thanks and an autographed copy of the book.

Now my admission: These experiences do not make me either a theologian or a scholar. I confess to being no more than a serious and well-read student of Judeo-Christianity with a smattering of appreciation for several other major religious traditions. But several decades of study and rumination have left me with a number of strong convictions about religion in general and Christianity in particular.

First and most basic is that any and all recourse to supernaturalism must end—gradually, perhaps, but programmatically and consistently. And this applies both to quotidian practices like crossing oneself in the batter's box and such fundamental beliefs as Jesus' physical resurrection. And before crying "Heretic!" please note that the earliest of the New Testament authors rejected that incredible doctrine: see 1 Corinthians 15:35–44. The syllogistic argument is a bit slippery and one may have trouble with the paradox of a spiritual body, but Paul clearly and unapologetically denied what is perhaps Christianity's most celebrated miracle. Dom Crossan characterized the problem perfectly when he observed that whenever an angel appears in a story, we are dealing with myth. This is not to deny the usefulness of myth, of course. The two mutually contradictory creation myths we find in Genesis 1 and 2–3 are worthy of the careful study they demand, but they were not intended and cannot possibly be taken as historical records of events. In view of the largely secular culture of the West in the twenty-first century, any tradition that continues to insist on belief in propositions that are widely acknowledged to be untrue is signing its own death warrant.

Second and similarly corrosive is the opposite side of that coin—anthropomorphism. Attributing human characteristics and motives to the Deity is an understandable and even natural narrative strategy, but a dangerous one. According to Matthew 5:45, Jesus said, ". . . your Father in heaven . . . makes the sun rise on the evil and the good, and sends rain on the righteous and on the unrighteous." Luke is a bit more circumspect, for he says, ". . . the Most High (*upsistos*) . . . is kind to the ungrateful and the wicked" (6:35). Luke is usually closer to the gospel source Q, and today one might be tempted to render the saying, "the Tao is kind to the ungrateful and the wicked" or "nature does not play ethical favorites". In any case, Jesus' use of personification could as well reflect contemporary usage as theistic conviction. That being the case, we may cut ourselves and our neighbors a bit of slack in such matters. Still, we need always to remember that since "gods" and "God" are concepts created by human minds, we might do well to give a thought to Luke's example. Whenever we attribute will, purpose, favoritism, or agency to a Deity, we are employing projection and risking blasphemy.

And that points up the need to reassess our notion of divinity.

From gods to God

Friedrich Nietzsche's proposal that grammar was the ultimate source of the idea of God may have a good deal of validity. One important difference between "The wind destroyed our olive trees" and "A bear killed our brother" is that we can see a bear. And since our earliest ancestors were no doubt inclined to attribute agency to a visible person, animal, or object, it is likely that they would imagine the wind or thunder—or conversely the beneficent sun and rain—to be initiated by some sort of invisible but very powerful being. Even today, as Lloyd Geering has observed, a small child who bumps into the sharp corner of a piece of dining room furniture is likely to accost the "naughty table" as the cause of the pain. And surely one can imagine how a crude idol intended to protect from danger or assure fertility could over millennia develop into Thor or Zephyrus, Siva or Ceres. We humans have created many gods.

We must also recognize that no tradition is entirely consistent in its invention of divinities. The nominal monotheism of the Hebrew Bible becomes problematic when we discover that the "One God" went by many names and was known by a number of quite different characteristics. Among the less common are El Shaddai (God Almighty), El Elyon (God Most High), El Roi, Yahweh Sabaoth (God of Armies) and the rare title Kinsman of Isaac (Genesis 31:42, 53).

But even the two most common appellations raise difficult issues because of the syncretic nature of Judaism. The unpronounceable YHWH of the Yahwist source can walk in the Garden of Eden with Adam and Eve, afterwards decide to destroy humankind, and still later promise his chosen people eternal ownership of their homeland. Meanwhile, the deity of the Elohist and Priestly sources (paradoxically named Elohim, Hebrew for "gods") was the one who created the universe, kept Abimelech from sleeping with Abraham's wife, and inspired Joseph's interpretation of dreams. And this variously portrayed God was also the divine Being who ordered Joshua's genocide of the Canaanites and who, after Israel suffered centuries of foreign oppression, was believed to have promised his battered people an Anointed One. (In Hebrew that is *Meshiach*, we say "Messiah", and the Greek word is "Christos".) It was he whom God would send to re-establish the dynasty of David and Solomon. Alas, it was a dream that could not come true.

It should be further noted that biblical authors not only testified to different names for the purportedly one God but accepted the existence of other gods. A henotheistic theology—the belief that the gods worshipped by different peoples have sovereign power within their territories—is evident in 2 Kings 3:4–27 and 5:1–19, written about 850 BCE. In the first, an Israelite army walks away from a certain victory when the king of Moab sacrifices his eldest son to the Moabite god Chemosh. Even Yahweh must bow to the power of a sovereign turf-holder who is obliged to respond appropriately to a loyal subject. In the second, the prophet Elisha understands that Yahweh's curative power can be imagined to travel to Syria in a few cubic feet of good Israelite dirt, and even permits the converted Naaman to feign allegiance to the local god Rimmon. No doubt this reflects a more sophisticated henotheism, for the prophet's humanity and spiritual authority have replaced mere superstition.

Before such early quasi-historical accounts as 1&2 Samuel and 1&2 Kings, the popular conception of gods seems to have been considerably less spiritual. The story of Rachel stealing the family idols to take them to her new home with Jacob's people does not suggest a highly evolved monotheistic theology. And Dominic Kirkham's discussion of the recent discovery of a ninth-century caravan stop is even more revealing. On the walls were inscriptions invoking both El and Baal, and seeking the protection of "Yahweh of Samaria and his Asherah" (that is, consort or wife). It would seem that a century before Elisha neither monotheism nor masculinity had exclusive bragging rights in the theological game.[4]

The point of all this is not to disparage the Bible for contradicting itself (which it does over and over again), but to show that it consists of a large number of transcripts and original compositions that represent the visions, beliefs, and proclamations of scores of people of different cultures and worldviews over a span of some three thousand years. In short, the Bible is not so much a book as a library. But how often has the Pulpit taken the trouble to inform the Pews that Genesis 1 was composed thousands of years after the origin of the mythic tales that comprise Genesis 2 and 3? How often reminded the flock that human attempts to conceptualize the causes—or a divine Cause—behind all phenomena and observed events have produced widely divergent and often irreconcilable results? Are believers aware that whether Israel's monotheism owes more to Akhenaten or Zoroaster, it was an idea whose time had come? Have they been told about Karl Jaspers and his axial Age hypothesis—that between 800 and 200 BCE several of today's worldwide religious traditions began replacing the profusion of national and tribal cults known only to those of a specific area or ethnic group? More pertinent yet, how many regular church-goers are aware that the book of Isaiah is a combination of three very different texts that reflect three very different historical

---

4. Kirkham, From Monk to Modernity, p. 36.

settings and religious themes? And do they know that the earliest one contains an historical datum mistranslated 800 years later to claim for Jesus divine origins at least as impressive as Caesar's[5]—or that the author of the second section, writing two centuries after the first, hailed the Persian emperor Cyrus as God's messiah?[6] In short, to what degree are Christians reasonably well informed about the history and content of the Bible and the religion to which they profess allegiance? One also wonders to what degree they are aware that as Charlie Hedrick, one of the leading scholars who gave us the Nag Hammadi library, put it: "In matters both large and small the canonical gospels contradict each other."[7]

---

5. Isaiah 7:14—the Hebrew alma (young woman) was rendered by the ambiguous Greek parthenos, and in English rendered "virgin", the Hebrew for which is bethula. The woman referred to was probably Ahaz' wife. And Julius Caesar's purported descent from Aeneas and Venus likely had less cachet than being son of the Almighty.

6. Isaiah 45:1.

7. Hedrick, The Wisdom of Jesus, p. 193.

A Popular Highjacking

Karen Armstrong has recently reminded us that a call for compassion is central to all of today's major religions. Her earlier magisterial study of the Axial Age, *The Great Transformation*, shows that recognition of the need to put an end to violence was a primary motive in that worldwide sea-change in religion between 800 and 200 BCE—the nexus of which is epitomized in the 2500-year-old dictum of Confucius we know as the Golden Rule. And she gives the hypothesis new meaning and urgency by observing that in today's world we must learn to apply this iconic maxim globally.

I think it is reasonable to propose that one of the primary functions of religion is to control our most powerful drive—the will to survive. It is, of course, both innate and essentially self-centered, but humankind's development of the cerebral cortex has led to evolving patterns of thought and behavior that transcend those of the rest of the animal world. To be sure, our selfish urgings have often led to almost unimaginable deeds of inhumanity. As James Madison observed in a famous 1785 tract, the history of religion is filled with episodes of "superstition, bigotry, and persecution."[8] Nevertheless, examples of magnanimity, altruism, and even self-sacrifice have made it possible to imagine that *homo sapiens* might one day be compelled—if only by the desire to survive—to make compassion the criterion of socially acceptable deportment.

But as Armstrong also observes, the demands of valid religions render them highly vulnerable to highjacking. We are all too familiar with the deeds of those who commandeer a conveyance or social movement intended to get us from point A to point B and redirect it to point C. Desperate migrants force the crew of a ship returning them to Libya to land them in Italy; authoritarian elements within a political or religious party take over a nascent progressive movement and begin to rule by dictate. A valid spirituality—a phenomenon that Plato correctly defined as a form of commitment—is too often trivialized into a rigid system of beliefs and rituals. In the Christian tradition it is an old story: Jesus himself noted that folks were quick to cry "Lord, Lord" but failed to follow his teaching (Luke 6:46). And the serious highjacking of his message began very early under the leadership of Paul of Tarsus—ironically known as "St. Paul." Whereas Jesus offered a better life on earth for those

---

8. Fortunato, Stephen J. Jr., "The dangers of religious exceptionalism", The Providence Journal, 10/7/21.

9

who practiced love of neighbor and even enemy, in Romans 10:9 Paul promised to Jew and Gentile alike eternal life in heaven if they would but profess Jesus' divinity (Rom 10:9)—a notion the Master would surely have considered blasphemous. Naturally, Paul won the contest for followers hands down, for both his product and his price were much more attractive.

The early contest for converts is amply documented: Peter's acceptance of dietary reform was attacked by the Jerusalem conservatives (Acts 11:1–3ff.); Paul branded him a hypocrite (Gal. 2:11–14); "James" launched an epistolary attack on Paul's "faith alone" doctrine (Jas. 2:14–20); and several indications in Paul's letters show that "spies" from Jerusalem attempted to sabotage his Gentile mission. In succeeding centuries "Church Fathers" like Athanasius and Arius assailed one another over theological and grammatical quibbles until Constantine's desire for political harmony led to the Council of Nicea, a masterpiece of compromise by which the emperor and the church sold out to one another. And through the centuries from Nicea to "the Troubles" in Ireland, selfish desire for power, money, and status have fueled faith-based conflicts. And that bland indictment glosses over the unspeakable horrors of the Crusades, the Inquisition, and centuries of anti-Semitism—to say nothing of centuries of religious wars, oppression, and extermination in Europe and criminal colonial adventures all around the world.

But even more spiritually perverse is the seldom mentioned fact alluded to above that within twenty or thirty years of Jesus' crucifixion the creedal and ritual center of gravity of the Christian tradition began to shift from a universal love that would establish God's kingdom among all peoples to a belief system that assured the faithful an afterlife of eternal bliss. The religion of Jesus had become a salvation cult centered on his mythic *alter ego*, Christ.[9] It may seem an impious exaggeration to suggest that Christianity has been in large measure a program of throwing Jesus under the bus to win believers by holding out the hope of a happy-ever-after; but however outrageous that proposition may at first appear, the time has come to give it careful consideration.

---

9. Former monk and priest Dominic Kirkham put it more elegantly: "Once Adam is no longer seen as an historical figure, the whole drama of salvation described by Paul in his letter to the Romans is undermined, and the whole soteriological edifice collapses—salvation history, Christ as redeemer and saviour, and the church as the instrument of salvation. We are left with Jesus as the counter-prophet of a radical way of life, and with the personal challenge of his ethical idealism." (personal correspondence)

A Highjacked Messiah

Jesus lived at a time when the Children of Israel were not on a winning streak. About the only time they ever had been was during the seven decades from about 1000 to 931 BCE, under the short-lived monarchy of David and Solomon. Prior to that they had been enslaved in Egypt or fighting for survival in Palestine. Thereafter they split into the nations of Judah and Israel; and with the exception of Israel's brief flowering under Omri—all but ignored by the biblical author because of the king's heterodoxy—struggled to attain independence due to constant local wars and successive defeats by Egypt, Assyria, Babylon, Greece, and Rome. It is no wonder, then, that over the centuries they evolved the myth that someday their God would relent and appoint for his chosen people another king, a descendant of David, who would once again rule over a sovereign nation and make it a beacon to all the world. This divinely chosen monarch, God's Anointed One, would rid the land of foreign conquerors and usher in a Messianic age.

As noted earlier the Greek for "anointed" is *christos*, and it was not until after Jesus' death that some of his followers began dressing him in that borrowed robe.[10] Alas, it was a very poor fit for several reasons. For one thing, he was born in Nazareth, a town in Galilee, an area into which Assyria had several centuries earlier transplanted a Gentile population. In fact, "galilee" means "district": it was known as the district of the Gentiles, and as such hardly the place to find a descendant of David. Indeed, identifying someone as a Galilean commonly implied "stupid Galilean" (cf. John 1:46). Nor was there any likelihood that after his symbolic attack on the Temple the Jewish priesthood would be inclined to anoint him as the people's savior. Worse yet, it was obvious that instead of his getting rid of the Romans, they executed him as a criminal and his followers scattered. And when late in the first century Matthew and Luke concocted their incredible and mutually contradictory genealogies and birth stories, descent from David became both dubious and contrary to the claim of divine paternity—the latter especially difficult for Jewish followers to accept.

In short, any attempt to conflate the Galilean teacher/prophet who died on a Roman cross and the Christ/Messiah of the myth of the long-awaited deliverer of Israel is not only an exercise in futility, but constitutes a radical distortion of Jesus' teaching.

---

10. Sanders, E. and Pelikan, J.J. Jesus. *Encyclopedia Britannica*, January 14, 2021. https://www.britannica.com/biography/Jesus.

The God Problem—cont'd.

At this point I sense a need to return to the issue of the super-naturalism and anthropomorphism that has infected Christian theology. Etymologically, of course, that word means simply "God talk"; and the way most Christians think and talk about the divinity they claim to revere is fraught with problems. At the root of the difficulty is the simple fact that reifying the characters of a supernatural order created by the human imagination involves one or two unsustainable presuppositions. A corollary to this is that advances in human knowledge have made it all but axiomatic that the universe is, as Don Cupitt puts it, "outsideless." Any god or God we humans create cannot be separate from nature, but part of it. Accordingly, the traditional theistic God of the Judeo-Christian dispensations is no longer a useful concept.

In his classic examination of spirituality, *The Varieties of Religious Experience*, William James aptly defined 'God' as "the unseen order of things"—a phrase I believe can be rendered in common parlance as "the way things are." But of course things are always changing! As Lloyd Geering has often reminded us, we no longer live in the three-decker universe assumed by the writers of scripture. Galileo issued the first wake-up call, but we know how religious leaders dealt with that. They stumbled on for another two centuries, devoutly ignoring the Renaissance and the Enlightenment, until seriously challenged by Christian scholars in the mid-nineteenth century. Christian God-talk might have undergone a profound evolutionary change when Ludwig Feuerbach postulated that "theology is anthropology" and persuasively argued that we humans were not created by God, but had ourselves created the thousands of unseen divinities that have been imagined over the millennia. Next, he and David Friedrich Strauss proposed that the doctrine of the incarnation applied not to Jesus alone, but to all of humankind, and Strauss took up the task of separating the historical Jesus from the gospel myths. But the self-serving defenders of an outmoded order again swept these new ideas under a thick ecclesiastical rug and nothing much changed.

During the next century it became increasingly difficult to ignore the modern world. In 1923 Martin Buber rang changes on two of Feuerbach's themes by contending that in accepting the inherent and ultimate worth of others we create and discover a transcendent quality of being. By 1930 Rudolf Bultmann had formulated his existential interpretation of Christianity, and by 1945 had shown the gospel accounts of Jesus' life to be so clearly mythical that depicting the historical Jesus was impossible. In 1949 Karl Jaspers produced his Axial Age theory, which has helped us to see that individual religious traditions evolve out of sweeping cultural changes, and do not reflect divine revelations. In 1960 Anglican Bishop John A. T. Robinson had the audacity to point out the flaws of traditional theology in his best-selling *Honest to God*, and by then Paul Tillich had persuaded thousands of his readers that 'God' does not exist (i.e. is not a separate entity or being), but rather is the ground or source of all being. In 1967 the Rev. Lloyd Geering, the Principal of New Zealand's Presbyterian Seminary, was charged with doctrinal error and disturbing the peace and unity of the church. These charges stemmed from his insistence that Jesus' resurrection was not an historical event, but a spiritual commitment, and that God was not a person, but a projected symbol of humankind's highest ideals and aspirations. The charges were dismissed, but many of the "faithful"—both lay and clergy—were outraged.

In 1993 Gordon Kaufman's *In Face of Mystery* picked up Buber's emphasis on relationship: his hypotheses of "self-reflexivity" and "feedback loops" speak to our ability to learn to relate fully and responsibly to ourselves and others, discovering at last the freedom of transcendent selflessness that reflects a potential for the sacred. Also, in 1993 the Westar Institute's Jesus Seminar issued a report of its seven-year study by over one hundred theology professors and clergy, all of them highly qualified scholars; in their considered opinion, 18% of the sayings attributed to Jesus in the gospels are authentic reports or show only minor evidence of authorial editing. The other 82% ranged from dubious to entirely fictitious. In 1997 their assessment of the historicity of the reported events of his life yielded the same judgment. God-talk, it seemed, was not always as we had supposed. In fact, a year later Episcopal Bishop John Shelby Spong published another ecclesiastical wake-up call: *Why Christianity Must Change or Die: A Bishop Speaks to Believers in Exile.* Lloyd Geering accorded it glowing praise and followed six years later with a brief sequel: *Is Christianity Going Anywhere?* It might also be noted that in this new millennium a growing number of Christian theologians and ministers are self-identifying as "non-theists" and even "atheists"—the former being a less abrasive but etymologically equal term.

And those with a bit of etymological curiosity may be intrigued by Prof. John D. Caputo's dictum: "God does not *exist*; God *insists*." ("Exist" derives from the Latin *exsistere*, to stand apart from; "insist" from *insistere*, to stand on or within.) On a similar note, I am reminded of a wise old lady who recalled that when a girl of only eight years it suddenly occurred to her that "God did not create the world, he just came along with it." (Wouldn't those two quotes provide raw material for a couple of interesting sermons?)

Unfortunately, I think, it's a pretty safe bet that the vast majority of today's churchgoers are largely or totally uninformed of such evolutionary (or revolutionary?) ideas. The reason, of course, is that the clergy—whose duty it should be to inform, instruct, and counsel them in matters of personal faith—are either blissfully unaware of what has been going on for the last several centuries or have decided not to broach such issues lest anyone take umbrage at the expression of an opinion that might ruffle some feathers.

Let me put the case even more bluntly: Since the early 1800s more than a dozen major Christian scholars have sought to render their ancient and inspiring tradition amenable to the modern world, but those who preach and teach the message seem to have paid them little or no heed. Rare indeed are sermons on Spong's Twelve Theses, Bultmann's demythological approach to the Gospels, or Marcus Borg's call to replace theism with panentheism. Rarer still, I suspect are Bible study groups who have wrestled with the Jesus Seminar's challenging conclusions. Since the clergy programmatically overlook such issues, could it be that their avoidance of new ideas has contributed to a growing sense of the irrelevance of religion that has long been emptying pews and closing churches?

Taking God's Name in Vain—a Colloquial Problem

From an early age most of us have been told to avoid this practice, but because we have forgotten what it originally meant, we have fallen into careless habits of God-talk. We personify and anthropomorphize the Deity so often and so carelessly that we trivialize the ineffable mystery that the symbol "God" represents, and we talk about imaginary things as if they were real. Only last evening the narrator of a television documentary on the Holy Land said that Jews, Christians, and Muslims alike consider no place on earth closer to Heaven than Jerusalem. But in 1999—more than two decades ago!—Pope John Paul II, a well-regarded conservative theologian, conceded that "Heaven is not a *place*; it is a state of mind." Or one might say that this ideal realm is yet another element of the mythical superstructure of Christianity—like everlasting life or the empty tomb—that we can't seem to stop treating as an objective or historical reality. I say "another" because we continue to demean God by envisioning "him" as an oriental monarch on steroids—all-knowing, all-powerful, all-loving, and supremely righteous. (Of course the frequency of disaster and tragedy in the world is strong evidence that those qualities cannot be attributed to a single source.) And only last week Franklin Graham, son of the widely acclaimed Billy, appeared on a paid television advertisement to inform us that "Jesus Christ was God's chosen way of pardoning human sin." Really? The ruler of the universe could not forgive people for sometimes behaving in accordance with an inborn inclination to do wrong? He had to require his own son to serve as a blood sacrifice for their misbehaviors? What human parent would even consider such a moral travesty?

Another troubling theological convention is that those who claim to revere "him" continually ask for and apparently expect to receive special treatment in return for performing certain rituals that will assure "his" favor. Above all, it seems, they are fond of reminding "him" how wonderful "he" is ("How Great Thou Art") and offering "him" fulsome praise ("O, For a Thousand Tongues . . ."). Surely this is a hangover from ancient times, an unfortunate echo of the abject devotion ("O King, live forever!") that ancient earthly monarchs demanded of those over whom they held mortal sway. Is this a reasonable way for twenty-first century people to conceive of "God"? I don't recall any reports that Jesus urged his followers to bow and scrape and flatter "God" with honorific titles. His chosen appellation for the deity was "Abba"—"father", perhaps with the connotation "dad". Nor for that matter did he see himself as "king of kings" or any of the florid titles later bestowed on him, but simply as another Son of Adam. Could it be that our motive (conscious or unconscious) in offering praise (from the Latin *pretium*, esteem) to sacred figures is to increase the likelihood of having our prayer (from *precatio*, request) answered? Dare one note that *pretium* also means "bribe"? For that matter, if "God" is a symbol, a concept, an abstraction, then whom or what are we praising; and who or what hears our praise?

It is difficult to argue that we hold "God" in the highest esteem when we daily trivialize "his" name in such common phrases as "Oh, my God", "God only knows", "for God's sake", "God knows I tried", and many others. One might accept "God helps those who help themselves" if "God" is understood to mean "the way things are"; but that's not how it is usually intended. Much more usual, I suspect, is the suggestion that "God" takes note of everyone's effort level, and whenever appropriate presses a button to reward those whose diligence merits "his" support. In today's world such a scenario is simply ludicrous.

Carl Jech—a pastor as well as college teacher and chaplain—sees things quite differently; he says that theology needs to be understood as more like poetry than prose. In a similar vein the late Gordon Kaufman of Harvard Divinity School proposed that "we have created God as a reference point for everything." Such ideas demand serious reflection, the kind of disciplined thinking that results when we do our best to imagine a proper deity. But alas, we prefer to invent stories and creeds that reduce the Universal Spirit to a convenient source of gratification and reassurance. It's the all too human story of a tradition that began with comforting the afflicted and too soon abandoned the call to afflict the comfortable. The long and short of it is that whenever we attribute agency to "God"—that is, request or depict some action on "his" part— we demote the Deity to a human level and thus "take his name in vain."

In his final letter written about twenty-five years after the crucifixion, the first and most influential of the apostles announced to the burgeoning Christian movement that Jesus' tragic lynching did not result from his efforts to free his fellow Jews from the worldly oppression of the Jerusalem Temple and the Roman Empire, but from "God's" desire to free humankind from the fatal taint of Adam's sin.[11] That canard, however, was foisted upon Jesus' early followers by a fellow Jew who must have known that Jewish tradition saw the story of the Fall not as a revolt against the clearly henotheistic and anthropomorphic Jahweh. Rather it

---

11. Rom 5

was an etiological myth that differentiated between animals, humans, and gods in terms of moral awareness and immortality, and explained the reason for several inescapable realities of the human condition. Paul sought to confer on Jesus a status higher than that of the Roman emperor, but to do so he was obliged to deny (or conveniently overlook) a fundamental Torahic prohibition. For the Genesis account of Abraham's last-minute release from "God's" command to sacrifice his son clearly signified the Judaic abrogation of human sacrifice—especially, one would imagine, if it were "God" sentencing his "only begotten son" to death. But apparently that was not a crucial matter for Paul, since his mission was to Gentiles, who would not likely know he was selling them a flawed bill of goods like others he had peddled elsewhere.[12]

Here permit me a brief excursus on "immortality"—a word that appears nowhere in the Hebrew Bible. To be sure, the concept of life after death is implied in the story of Elijah's miraculous transportation into heaven (c. 850, see 2Kgs 2:11); though if taken to apply to ordinary mortals, any such belief was strongly condemned. That is, until after the Exile, when around 500 BCE Zoroastrian doctrines began to influence Judaism. Then, when in 167–164 bloody persecutions by Antiochus Epiphanes produced a flood of martyrdoms, the truly pious could not avoid concluding that a righteous God must reward those who died defending 'his' name by someday restoring them to life. And thus the way was prepared for Pharisaic Jews to believe in the afterlife denied by their Sadducee brothers (cf. Matt 22:23a) and for Jesus' early followers to proclaim his resurrection. It should also be noted that the phrase "eternal life" used repeatedly by the gospel writers is a mistranslation of *zoen aionion*, life in this age [or the one to come?], which implies a quality of life rather than its perpetuity.

As Lloyd Geering explains, Jesus' resurrection was not an historical event, but was and always is a spiritual one. And a recent story in the magazine of the Sea of Faith UK beautifully expressed the nature of the experience: "Mary, as we knew her form, is nowhere now. . . . [y]et, mention her name and she is straightway present through the spiritual power of love. It's just that we can't touch her anymore, and that is so sad."[13]

---

12. 1 Thess 4:14–17; Gal 1:8–9; 1Cor 11:23–26; 2 Cor 12:2–4. The dubious nature of these claims will be examined at some length in a later section.
13. Gilbert, Grenville, "Mary's Touch", *Sofia* #137, Sep. 2020, p. 10.

"Standing on the promises"—another "God talk" problem

It should be obvious that neither inclusion in an anthology of "sacred" writings, nor claims of "inspiration," nor being hailed as "Scripture" can guarantee either authenticity or accuracy. Scholars classify six of the thirteen letters that the Bible attributed to Paul as "pseudepigrapha"—a polite term for "forgeries." Genesis opens with two creation accounts that are totally different, and the two stories of Jesus' birth contradict one another on every point except the names of the three primary characters and the place of birth. But even that last detail is a fiction, for scholars today generally agree that he was born and raised in Nazareth. And they now recognize that the four canonical gospels—like the dozen or fifteen others that have been discovered—cannot be classified as history or biography, but are largely expressions of conviction or attempts at persuasion. Furthermore, the framers of the Christian Bible removed Jonah and Daniel from their Jewish place among "The Writings" and placed them with the prophetic books—a striking case of doctrinal interests distorting the meaning and intent of the authors. The lovely parable known as the Book of Ruth is similarly misplaced and its significance lost, for although set in about 1200 BCE, it is a bitter attack on Ezra's forcible dissolution of priestly marriages 800 years later. And one especially infamous passage, a patent fiction that would have been removed by a church more interested in honesty than perpetuating a disgraceful slander, is Matt 27:25. There a Jewish audience petitions Pilate for the release of a terrorist named Barabbas (son of the Father!) and accepts for themselves and their descendants any guilt for the shedding of Jesus' blood. Over the last two thousand years this abomination has led to the slaughter of millions of Jesus' fellow Jews, and yet I have never heard anyone inveigh against it! John Dominic Crossan, perhaps the most eminent of modern biblical scholars, recently published a book every serious Christian should be acquainted with: *How to Read the Bible and Still Be a Christian*. A widespread acquaintance with its many interesting revelations would do much to improve the quality of our mutual "God-talk", for most of those who specialize in that discourse have proved to have a much greater concern for man-made doctrine than for truth.

In summing up the shared conclusions of a three-day colloquium by seven outstanding scholars representing a highly diverse spectrum of religious traditions, Marcus Borg noted their common understanding that God is indefinable, not a being but a dimension of reality, and not an article of belief but an element of experience.[14]

Let a final word from Dom Kirkham epitomize the difficulty of engaging in serious "God-talk" in the twenty-first century:

> Insofar as God is the symbol of ultimate concern or order, or the embodiment of all that is connected to religion, modernity presents a particular challenge. To speak of God in a world of random natural selection that emerged billions of years ago as the product of . . . a previously collapsed universe and will end in entropic darkness, is to divest the word of any objective content or real meaning in the traditional sense. As a result modern talk about God has become confused by the often unrecognized dichotomy in the use of the word. On the one hand there is the subjective state of mind that enables us to create an overarching sense of meaning and purpose in life; on the other hand there is the nature of causality in the natural objective order. Perhaps the most disturbing feature of Modernity for me was the growing sense that what was once a seamless connection between these two realms had been severed.[15]

In short, it is long past time for each of us to be more careful in our "God-talk" and to call for a like degree of discretion on the part of others.

---

14. Borg & Mackenzie, eds., *God at 2000*, p. 159.
15. Kirkham, *From Monk to Modernity*, pp. 14–15.

Biblical Narratives

Perhaps that will serve as an unintended but appropriate point to begin a discussion of biblical narratives, a many-faceted subject that is too often overlooked or glossed over. The anthology we call *The Holy Bible* includes accounts that range from facts and figures to fairytale fantasies and reflects some three millennia of humankind's attempts to give meaning to experience. From Lamech's threat (Gen 4:23–24) to John's Gospel we find a record of reportage that both answers and provokes a myriad of questions.

As Art Dewey's opening epigraph suggests and the credo of the Sea of Faith movement insists, religion is a human creation. It attests to humankind's ongoing and ever-evolving attempt to discover and live in accordance with insights that derive from experiences that go beyond the surly facts of daily life and point to a transcendent level of existence. When we are ready to understand this, we can begin to see that theology's most appropriate medium is fiction and its modality is necessarily poetry—a word derived from the Greek *poiein*, to create.

The very ancient recognition of the narrative-poetic nature of religious expression is made strikingly clear in this explanation by Dr. Miriam-Rose Ungunmerr-Baumann, a contemporary Indigenous Australian artist and thinker:

> [The] name of my people means 'Deep Water Sounds' or 'Sounds of the Deep.' This talk is about tapping into that deep spring within us . . . The identity we have with the land is sacred and unique. Many people are beginning to understand this more. Also there are many Australians who appreciate that Aboriginal people have a very strong sense of community. All persons matter. All of us belong . . .
>
> [There is] another special quality of my people. I believe it is our most unique gift, the greatest gift we can give our fellow Australians. In our language this quality is called dadirri. It is inner, deep listening and quiet, still awareness . . .
>
> A big part of dadirri is listening. Through the years we have listened to our stories. They are told and sung, over and over, as the seasons go by. Today we still gather around the campfires and together we hear the sacred stories.
>
> As we grow older, we ourselves become the storytellers. We pass on to the young ones all they must know. The stories and songs sink quietly into our minds and we hold them deep inside. In the

ceremonies we celebrate the awareness of our lives as sacred. The contemplative way of dadirri spreads over our whole life. It renews us, brings us peace, and makes us whole again.

So let us then recall some of our old stories, remembering that every story creates a world as the teller sees it—or wishes it to be. Hence differing worldviews will result in many diverse pictures, genres, and levels of sophistication. Leading the procession is the narrative portrayal of Lamech with its suggestion of a world in which raw personal power is a basic element of survival. A number of scholars see his bluster as the oldest element of the textual tradition, predating the written version of the creation myth of Genesis 2–4—the oral composition of which was likely much earlier. And perhaps this is the place to repeat that Genesis 1 is a much later writing, dating to the post-exilic period and thus some six centuries later than the text of the Jahwist story of Adam and Eve.[16] And that chronological relationship is evident when one recognizes that the Garden of Eden story is clearly mythic in nature, while the creation of order from chaos is a sophisticated narrative which, as Lloyd Geering has often observed, is much like a modern "theory of everything".

At this point we might do well to list several of the narrative genres that are found in the Bible. **Myth** is one, and it appears many times in the earliest books of the Hebrew Bible (e. g. Noah's flood, the giving of the Law, and the Exodus) and at several key points in the Christian scriptures (the flight into Egypt, the divine announcement of Jesus' sonship, and Paul's assurance of substitutionary salvation). Obviously, thinking people in the twenty-first century must recognize these and many other reports as spiritual rather than historical in nature. Myths are narrative attempts to explain human experiences, to be sure, but their events could not have been recorded by video cameras (had such been present) or objectively validated by their claimants. Still, their importance must not be minimized, for they represent, confirm, inculcate, and indeed project the worldview and values that sustain a culture—that are capable of making us "whole again."

Somewhat later in the scriptural order—and the increasing complexity of humankind's intellectual and imaginative powers—we encounter **legends** with their human protagonists. Not that the distinction

16. According to the documentary hypothesis (q. v.), an evolving understanding of the origins of the Torah, that nucleus of the Hebrew scriptures reflects the compilation of four traditions: the Jahwist, Elohist, Deuteronomic, and Priestly—the first and earliest dated to c. 950 BCE and the last and latest to c. 350 BCE.

is clear and distinct, for Abraham's fiery encounter with the Lord is surely mythic, as is Joseph's rise to authority in Egypt, and Moses is the legendary hero of a national myth. Even Joshua, who carries out Jahweh's campaign of ethnic cleansing to make room in Canaan for the children of Israel, plays the dual role of man and mythic super-hero.

Only with the book of Judges do we meet legendary heroes, people who needed a bit of supernatural help to get the job done. Think of the self-confessed nonentity Gideon, who was able to carry out one of the last stages of the occupation of the land their God had promised them. (Note that a distinct aura of national myth remains.) And with the arrival of Samuel, Saul, David, and Solomon—along with the early prophets Elijah and Elisha—legend is beginning to blend with history, because kings tend to have a strong desire to have their exploits recorded. It's only a blend, to be sure, for we have two contradictory accounts of how David gained Saul's notice and rose to prominence. And neither the account of Samuel throwing Saul under the bus and anointing David—who at the time was running a protection racket in the Negev—nor the events of the protracted war between the two anointed kings have the earmarks of unbiased history.

Nor does God's uncritical favoritism for David seem to accord with the king's flagrant adultery and cold-blooded murder to cover it up. Nor does it seem objective history to depict David and Solomon as the builders of a great temple and palace in Jerusalem now that modern archaeologists cannot find a single stone of such a structure. Last of all, trumpeting Solomonic wisdom seems problematic when the record also shows that he sold a number of his northern town's subjects to the king of Lebanon to pay for building materials and craftsmen, and so oppressed the ten northern tribes of Israel that upon his death they revolted against his son. The result was two weak and often conflicting kingdoms, Judah in the south and Israel in the north—both of which ultimately fell to powerful neighboring empires and never regained true political independence. The textual result of the split is separate traditions, J and E, that often exhibit striking differences. Genesis 33:18 (E), for instance, records that Jacob obtained title to Shechem, later the Israelite capital, by purchase; Genesis 34 (J) offers an horrific tale of rape and massacre to explain how it came into his possession.

And though the two traditions agreed that the deity was merciful and forgiving (Exodus 34:6–7a), verse 7b says that Yahweh ". . . lets nothing go unchecked, punishing the father's fault in the sons and in the grandsons to the third and fourth generation" (Jerusalem Bible). Who changed the rules of the game? Can it be that someone had an interest in requiring temple sacrifice to appease a sometimes angry God? Originally sacrifice was a way of expressing thanks, showing gratitude for God's providence, but gradually it became a ritual aimed at gaining God's favor for future plans or atoning for past misbehavior. It seems difficult to ignore the difference between returning a small portion of blessings received and currying future favor or cancelling past sins by sprinkling the blood of animals on an altar. Of course the latter allows royal scribes and temple personnel to enjoy a high-protein diet . . .

Is it possible to discern in Samuel's selection of Saul—a handsome young rustic who "stood head and shoulders above everybody else"— a small, bubbling spring that eventually grew into the great river that dominates human history: the juncture of political and ecclesiastical power? It seems ironic that after Samuel's sons had proved themselves unfit (1 Sam 8:3), the old priest who had long judged over the children of Israel warned them against such a consolidation of power (1 Sam 8:11–18). And may we not see in his later rejection of Saul—was it due to David's popularity after he slew Goliath (1Sam 18:6–7) or the king's failure to carry out the Amalekite massacre (1 Sam 15:1–3 ff.) or both?— the inevitable rivulet that led from a politically active ecclesiastic to the Holy Roman Empire?

Nor is the Hebrew Bible alone in offering twisted **history**, for in the Christian scriptures credible historical narrative is almost equally hard to find. After many years of intense study and debate, Westar scholars concluded that of the sayings attributed to Jesus in the five major Gospels (Mark, Matthew, Luke, John, and Thomas) only 18% can be judged more or less authentic; and the depicted events of his life rate a similar judgment. The Westar scholars who later assessed the book of Acts found its reporting of events somewhat less accurate.

In short, the ostensibly historical records found in the Bible are so contaminated with scribal bias that they can seldom be taken at face value. So where does that leave the student of biblical narrative? Is the search for meaning a hopeless one? By no means! In fact, as noted earlier—and as the Rev Peter Catt, former Dean of Brisbane's St. John's Anglican Cathedral proposes—narratives are humankind's way of trying to make life itself meaningful. Not only that, but he argues that narrative traditions—"metanarratives"—are artifacts by which cultures create the worldviews that in turn shape our perception of reality.[17] Let us, then, look at a few well-known biblical stories whose value does not depend

---

17. Catt, "Scripture, Science, and the Big Story", *The Once and Future Scriptures*, Greg Jenks, ed.

on their historicity or even their accurate depiction of realty. Both fiction and fantasy are legitimate tools of those who seek goodness, truth, or inspiration. Shall we avoid the study of Jesus' parables because they were fictions? Shall we eschew exegesis of the book of Jonah because the author employed fantastic plot elements? Of course not. Rather let us adopt the criteria attributed by Chaucer to the fictitious Harry Bailey; a story is excellent to the degree it is both entertaining and edifying.

Old Testament Narratives

Jonah is as good a place as any to begin. First, let it be noted that the Christian scriptures have wrenched it from its original context. The Hebrew Bible includes it not in the Torah or the Prophets, but in a miscellaneous section called "The Writings." After all, Jonah was a sad example of a prophet, for upon receiving his call to prophecy, he tried to run and hide at the end of the earth. His commission was, to be sure, a challenging one—rather like sending a rabbi to Berlin in 1940 to convert the Third Reich. One further notes that the pagan sailors who strove mightily to save his life were better lovers of God and neighbor than he. The author had a fine sense of irony. And when our hero at last delivers his anachronistic oracle against Nineveh (in his day and that of his father Amittai, Nineveh was not the Assyrian capital, but a dusty crossroads town), he seems to omit the "unless" part of it (Jon 3:4, but see also 3:10). Still, the sophisticated Assyrians immediately know how to avoid destruction and initiate a crash program of expiation, leaving Jonah devastated: his threat proved false. So he sulks and fumes in the partial shade of a little stick-built hut, hoping against hope that God will make good on his (Jonah's) threat. Instead, God has a vine cover the hut and then suddenly shrivel and die. The punch line of the parable—for that's what this is—comes when God asks Jonah to weigh his sense of wounded pride against the lives of thousands of men, women, and innocent children—to say nothing of all their domestic animals! Anyone who cannot derive a spiritually edifying lesson from that droll little tale must never be allowed to violate a pulpit.

Another trenchant parable masking as history is the book of Ruth. Even more drastically anachronistic than Jonah, the story is set in the time of the judges (1200–1025 BCE), but the text must be dated to the time of Ezra (400–350 BCE), for it is clearly a protest against his inhumane dissolution of marriages between Temple functionaries and local women (Ez 10:16–44)—a program that condemned scores of innocent women and children to beggary, shame, and worse. The narrative is simple: Ruth, a Moabitess, is one of those with whom all Jews are forbidden by Torah (Dt 23:3–6) to have any dealings. Yet when a Jewish couple and their two sons are driven by famine to leave Bethlehem ("the house of bread"!) and settle in Moab, the sons marry local women; and when the husband and both sons die suddenly, his wife Naomi decides to return home, since the famine has passed. She advises her daughters-in-law to find new husbands in Moab, but Ruth will not leave her, and insists on adopting her people and religion. The reason, one must assume, is the powerful example of Naomi's character and faith. In short order Ruth pitches in to support her mother-in-law, and so impresses a wealthy relative that he marries her and they produce a son who, we are informed in the story's brief and dramatic denouement, was David's grandfather. So take that, Ezra: David's great-grandmother was a Moabite, and your strict orthodoxy was not reverence, but an abomination. Is it mere coincidence that another compelling lesson from the Jewish scriptures involves both anachronism and startling irony?

To suggest that more than chance is at work here, let us take note of another piece of Jewish story-telling that Christian editors incorrectly assigned to the prophetic category—the book of Daniel. The hero of this collection of fairytales was a legendary character of Hebrew lore, as anyone who is not limited to the King James Version is free to discover. Two accounts of his wisdom, "Susannah and the Elders" and "Bel and the Dragon" appear in the Jerusalem Bible (an impressive product of Roman Catholic scholarship) as Chapters 13 and 14 of a text that is clearly out of place between Ezekiel and Hosea. Let it also be noted in passing that in some compilations "Susannah" is Chapter 1, since here our hero appears as a mere lad who, already the equal of the best modern detective, is able to identify and convict a pair of corrupt elders and save an innocent female victim from a shameful death.

But all that is peripheral to the fantasies of this last-written and most precisely datable book of the Hebrew Bible. Written during the Great Persecution of 167–164 BCE by means of which Antiochus Epiphanes sought to eradicate Judaism, it employs miraculous fictions set in the early years of the Babylonian Exile. The obvious dual purpose of the stories and the 440–year anachronism was to assure its Jewish readers that God would save those who held fast to the faith of their fathers and to avoid repercussions by the present murderous autocrat. Just as he had saved Daniel from the lions and the fiery furnace, God would preserve his people, and substituting Nebuchadnezzar and Belshazzar for Antiochus would render the message clear to its Jewish audience but opaque to the Greek oppressor. No doubt due to the more than four century time warp, the text presents a patchwork of times, settings, and characters—including an invented Persian monarch—and for some reason the Hebrew switches to Aramaic from 2:4 to the end of chapter 7 before returning to Hebrew thereafter.

Nonetheless, Daniel is a fine example of the use of narrative fiction to serve spiritual as well as political aims, for it no doubt helped fuel the Maccabean revolt that toppled Antiochus and led to a turbulent period of political independence under high priests or kings from 134 to 63 BCE. And the Maccabean period (164–134) was the setting for one final example of contemporary Jewish historical narrative that may have been the source of Christianity's central narrative. Chapter 7 of 2 Maccabees, a deuterocanonical book included in Catholic Bibles but not in the Authorized Version of 1611, recounts the story of a family martyrdom that deserves to be better known—but the grisly details of which those of a sensitive nature might do well to avoid.

Greek enforcers of Antiochus Epiphanes' anti-Jewish edicts commonly offered recalcitrant Jews the choice of eating pork or suffering a painful death. In chapter 6 a revered nonagenarian teacher of the Law was bludgeoned to death after spitting out the forbidden meat, and in the following chapter seven sons are in their mother's presence brutally tortured for refusing to ingest the prohibited portion. Each in turn expresses his loyalty to God's law: as he dies the next invokes ". . . God's promise that we shall be raised up . . ."; and as the seventh nears death his mother assures him that ". . . the creator of the world . . . will most surely give you back both breath and life, seeing that you now despise your own existence for the sake of his laws." Finally, after 'the seven Maccabees' died ". . . with perfect trust in the Lord", their mother was put to death. But their dying condemnations were fulfilled, for not long afterwards Judas Maccabeus led a successful revolt that culminated in the persecutor's gruesome death and the cleansing and rededication of the Temple. To be sure, the author pulled out all the rhetorical stops in presenting a no doubt exaggerated account, but the historical core is authentic.

More important for the present purpose is the fact that this text contains the earliest example of Jewish acceptance of belief in bodily resurrection. Judaism had long rejected the idea, holding that only God is immortal; note that Adam and Eve were driven from Eden not for what they had done, but for what they might do (Gen 3:22). No doubt this radical theological revision resulted largely from Greek persecution, but the seeds were planted during the Exile, when Zoroastrian eschatological doctrines gained a degree of acceptance. At any rate, while the traditionalist Sadducees denied resurrection (see e. g. Matt 22:23), Judaism's doctrine of corporate salvation was beginning to waver; in fact, the liberal Pharisaic acceptance of individual judgment and a personal afterlife was apparently growing in popularity—note the words placed on Jesus' lips in Matthew 22:30. In a world where life for all but a very small minority was, as Thomas Hobbes put it, "nasty, brutish, and short," the promise of a happy ever after surely had a powerful appeal.

And within a decade or two after the crucifixion, Paul had persuaded a growing throng of Gentiles that that not only was salvation possible, but that God had sent his son to be the blood sacrifice that alone could make it available.

At this juncture a few contextual points need to be made. First, as early as 50 CE severe tensions had arisen between Paul's Gentile mission and the "Jesus Jews" of the Jerusalem community led by Jesus' brother James and the apostle Peter. Not only had Paul been "poaching" God-fearers—non-Jews residing in the Roman provinces who found a spiritual home in Judaism (Matt 8:5–10)—but an increasing number of unaffiliated Gentiles were attracted by Paul's decision to eliminate circumcision and a number of other rituals and practices (Rom 3:28–30). To the "Pillars" of the mother church this was nothing less than blatant heresy, and as we learn from Paul's own letters they sent emissaries to undermine his teachings and disrupt his churches (Gal 2:11–13). This already disruptive situation was gravely exacerbated by the Jewish Rebellion of 66–70, which resulted in the destruction of the Temple and Rome's wholesale slaughter of Jews and Christians alike. And Mark was written in the immediate aftermath of this catastrophe, to be followed in a decade or two by Matthew and Luke. It is all but certain, then, that Matthew 22:30, with its allusion to resurrection, is the evangelist's creation rather than an authentic report. And this is all the more likely since as a Galilean, Jesus probably had little contact or even familiarity with Pharisees or their beliefs—though scholars generally agree that his doctrines and teachings had much in common with their views. Accordingly, his virulent maledictions of "scholars and Pharisees" in Mathew 23 (the most Jewish of the gospels) are often seen as anachronisms reflecting the postwar efforts of those loyal to Torah to keep Pauline Christians from converting Jews to their new dispensation.

An excursus
Pauline fictions

To keep our overview of biblical fiction chronologically correct, we must for a time turn back from gospel to epistle and examine several of Paul's creations. In doing so we omit all but the most cursory mention of three texts that are of vital importance in understanding the Christian tradition: the Gospel of Thomas, the Q Gospel or Sayings Source, and the Didache; but since they have little or no narrative content and their dates likely overlap with those of the canonical gospels, they must await further mention. Paul's dates are fairly firm, and his employment of fiction did much to shape what we call Christianity. His earliest letter, 1 Corinthians, is generally dated 50–51—although such well-regarded scholars as John Knox and Gerd Lüdemann place it a decade earlier—and his last, Romans, could be as early as 53–54 or as late as 57–58.

And while his epistles are largely pastoral in nature—encouragement and remonstrance, warning and exhortation, advice and reassurance—their rather few narrative elements tend to be brief. Still, in his letter to the Roman community—one he did not found and had never visited, but clearly was eager to win over to his doctrines—he sets forth the Christian metanarrative of salvation history: the divine Christ sent as a sacrifice to overcome the taint of Adam's disobedience. This is, of course, the meta-myth that provided the foundation for all of traditional Christianity; but it is equally clear that its elements cannot be found in the recorded teachings of Jesus. Hyam Maccoby's title says it all: *The Mythmaker: Paul and the Invention of Christianity*—the story that shaped the world of western civilization for two thousand years!

Of admittedly lesser importance but nonetheless vital to the robust permanence of the Pauline edifice are four other narrative claims by which the self-anointed Apostle sought to defuse specific crises that threatened the unity or even the future of three of his churches. To be sure, these claims might have passed muster in the first century and with their particular audiences, but the evidence they put forth cannot be taken at face value in today's world. And perhaps it should be noted in his defense that Paul was consumed and driven by his visionary experience near Damascus, and had no direct contact with Jesus and apparently little knowledge or even interest in his life or teachings. Absent the facts, one is obliged to improvise.

29

1 Thessalonians 4:13–18

It seems clear that during his founding visit to this community, Paul had promised or strongly implied that Jesus' second coming was imminent, indeed within the lifetime of all present, whereupon he would reward all who were faithful believers by taking them with him up to heaven. (Apparently this was not a unique doctrine—see Mark 9:1—but it cannot be attributed to Jesus.) Unfortunately, Paul learned, some members of his Thessalonian congregation had died while he was away, and some of those still alive were murmuring that Paul had sold them a bill of goods. The church was in trouble. His response was a letter, much of which was devoted to praising the community for its constancy and high repute in the broader Christian brotherhood; but near the end he included a sort of off-handed reassurance: *Oh, by the way, if any are worried about not being included when the Lord takes us all to Heaven with him,* **he personally assured me** *that all the faithful will be so rewarded.* The problem appears in verse 15: "For this we declare to you by the word of the Lord . . ." If Paul is seen to claim an oral promise, that is a false statement; if he refers to a visionary experience, by modern criteria he is at best fudging the facts. At any rate, Jesus was not the source of the popular but clearly impossible 'Rapture' narrative. Lüdemann traces it to a Jewish apocalyptic myth, though he allows it might have been a Pauline invention[18] but in either case it is a fabricated attempt to avoid an ecclesiastical and apostolic disaster.

Galatians 1:11–12

As was the case in Thessalonica, not only did local pagan resistance to Paul's essentially Jewish message have an unsettling effect on his community, but emissaries from the "Mother Church" in Jerusalem attacked him for eliminating traditional Jewish practices and observances.[19] And clearly these issues were having a disruptive effect, for he begins his letter by claiming divine sanction and in 3:1 calls his Galatian flock (pick your favorite translation) "clueless," "foolish," or "stupid." Why? Because, he says, they are "turning to a different gospel—not that there is another gospel" (1:6–7). That is, his interpretation of what might be called 'the Jesus phenomenon' is the only correct one, and anyone who says otherwise is accursed (1:7–9). And whence his authority for this harsh judgment? He ". . . received it through a revelation of Jesus Christ" (New

---

18. Lüdemann, Gerd, *The Earliest Christian Text*, pp. 53–54.

19. Many would no doubt have found Jewish dietary restrictions a problem, and circumcision would have been as especially difficult "sell" to Greco-Roman males.

Revised Standard Version, v. 12). A recent translation by a group of four Westar scholars is a bit more amenable to the modern ear: ". . . it came to me as an insight from God about Jesus as God's Anointed."[20] Even this claim, however, presupposes a supernatural source and amounts to a special pleading that preemptively disallows critical analysis. To many in the first century invoking the Almighty might have carried the day, but Jesus himself would almost certainly have found Paul's arrogation to be presumptuous if not downright blasphemous.

2 Corinthians 12:2–4

Here again, as in Thessalonica and Galatia, the future of Paul's missionary effort has been threatened by so-called "re-judaizers." These were emissaries from the Jerusalem community whose leaders—the "pillars" to whom Paul refers in his earlier claim to have received their blessing (Gal 2:6–9)—have come to see his rejection of Jewish traditions as heretical. And this is no mild attack to be shrugged off by an "Oh, by the way" response or an assurance that "My understanding that Jesus' death and resurrection was a game-changing event in human history is the only true gospel." For this time the challenge is personal: the troublemakers who have come to Corinth are claiming not only that Paul lacks the bearing and charisma of a true prophet, but that his doctrines and credentials are inferior to theirs. And clearly Paul is feeling the heat, for he finds it necessary to counter their disparagements with a self-deprecating shtick on boasting, the climax of which is an oblique but unmistakable claim to have been taken up to heaven and afforded a revelatory experience so ineffable that it cannot be revealed.

In this brief narrative he has played the ultimate and unassailable "God-card," a preemptive move that may well have saved the day in 57 CE, but is difficult to take seriously in 2021.

1 Corinthians 11:17–30

In this passage we have what may well be Paul's most flagrant example of employing a narrative fiction to enforce a doctrinal teaching. It is all the more extraordinary for three reasons: because he must have known the report was untrue, because it employs narrative misinformation to deal with a pastoral crisis, and because the narrative core of the story became the iconic and defining ritual of all but a very few Christian traditions. Oddly enough, the problem arose not from the need to enforce a theological doctrine or avoid an ecclesiastical schism,

---

20. Dewey et al., *The Authentic Letters of Paul*, p. 52.

but over what would seem a relatively minor social issue: appropriate behavior when the community gathered for weekly worship.

These meetings included both a liturgical service featuring a symbolic reenactment of Jesus' putative last supper, and a communal dinner—a repast that might be the only full meal some members would enjoy that week, and thus an important aid to Paul's missionary efforts. But the more affluent worshippers had gotten into the habit of coming early, getting most of the good food, bringing along a bottle of nice wine to share with friends, and failing to associate with their less fortunate fellow-believers. Thus the community—the body of Christ—was being torn apart, and unity must be restored. Worse yet, Paul said, this desecration of the body and blood of Christ had caused illnesses and even deaths.

The only cure was a scrupulous observance of the communion ritual he had taught them, a reprise of Jesus' final meal with the disciples during which the covenant of bread and wine was established as a reminder of his sacrifice. The story of this ritual and its significance, Paul assured them, he had received from the Lord.

But this is a fiction that only a Gentile could believe. A Jew would find repulsive the idea that a Jewish teacher would call on his Jewish followers to ingest blood and engage in cannibalism—even if only symbolically. But Paul was a Jew! How could he have created such a story? No wonder that Jesus' relatives and followers in the Jerusalem church sought to stamp out Paul's heretical adventures.

Where can such a scenario have originated? It might have derived in part from the two Eucharistic texts recorded in the Didache. But only in part, for they were, as the term indicates, thanksgiving rituals, and one of them names David and Jesus in parallel as givers of the loaf and the cup. Even more to the point, neither makes any mention of sacrifice. Or one might invoke similarities in the rites of the many popular miracle and mystery cults of that time—those of Isis, Dionysus, Magna Mater, and Mithra are likely candidates. Better yet, perhaps, is the traditional Roman memorial banquet in which symbolic elements were eaten and drunk to infuse the participants with the virtues of the hero being honored.

Whatever Paul's source or sources, the result was a fictitious story that was adopted by the authors of Mark, Matthew, and Luke and eventually became the Roman Catholic Mass, the Anglican Eucharist and the Protestant Communion. It might be noted in passing that in John's gospel the Last Supper is omitted, and in its place we have Jesus washing his disciples' feet. And I for one find it interesting that Quakers commonly replace Communion with a monthly Potluck meal (how historically appropriate!) and that in 1832 Ralph Waldo Emerson felt obliged to resign his pastorate at Boston's Second Church because he would not lead the Communion service. "This mode of commemorating Christ is not suitable to me," he said.

But now, having laid a number of serious charges against the self-appointed apostle from Tarsus, I am obliged by the rules of honest discourse to reveal known evidence for the defense. Here, then, are the two best arguments I know.

The first I have borrowed from Bob Price, an occasionally quirky but brilliant Westar scholar whose penetrating essay "Can We Still Teach Biblical Moral Values?" makes the useful point that although all moral wrongs are unholy, not all ritually unclean acts are immoral. "[Paul] still quotes scripture with enthusiasm when it comes to morality. But kosher laws? Circumcision? Holy days? Take them or leave them, says the Apostle to the Gentiles."[21]

It may well be that what earned Paul the opprobrium of the Jerusalem "pillars" was precisely that which allowed his admittedly warped view of Jesus to spread beyond Judaism to the rest of the Greco-Roman world and become so central to Western culture that it survived until a more enlightened age could begin to better appreciate its timeless truth.

Of equal if not greater importance was his radical proclamation of equality: "There is no longer Jew or Greek, there is no longer slave or free, there is no longer male and female; for all of you are one in Christ Jesus" (Gal 3:28). Paul may have borrowed the wording, but this formula made specific the revolutionary exhortations of the Galilean teacher who had paid with his life for preaching universal love and compassion. Indeed, so radical were its demands that Paul's own disciples later added contradictory assertions to his letters (see e. g. 1 Cor 14:34–35).[22] They even went so far as to include in their own forged letters (Eph, Col, 1&2 Tim, Tit) passages that softened or implicitly negated Paul's program of social revolution.[23]

That radicality, for which the world was not yet ready and still is not, must have been etched in Paul's conscience by his visionary experience, for it represented a daring footnote to Jesus' assertion of the moral

---

21. Miller, Robert J., ed., *The Future of the Christian Tradition*, pp. 214–215.
22. Walker, William O. Jr., *Some Surprises from the Apostle Paul*, pp. 97–100.
23. Crossan, John Dominic, *How to Read the Bible & Still Be a Christian*; ch. 14, "Paul and the Normality of Empire," pp. 219–233.

authority of God's law. For his good deeds, then, we may find it in our hearts to grant him partial absolution for fictions that for two millennia have led to grave and widespread misrepresentations of the teachings of Jesus.

And once again I yield to former priest and formidable paleographer Dominic Kirkham for a final word:

> By the time the New Testament was collated in the third century CE not only had the teaching of Jesus been significantly edited but the Hebraic cultural world, of which he was a part, had been destroyed: Jesus the Jew had become apotheosized into an Imperial Roman Lord. As for my initial conundrum concerning who founded Christianity, we can now see that St. Paul has the best claim. As for the historical Jesus, the Jewish *hassid* or holy man from Galilee who challenged and inspired his audiences with a radical message beyond expectation—might one say that much of him has been lost in translation?[24]

---

24. Kirkham, Dominic, "Lost in Translation?, *Sofia* December 2020, p.19.

New Testament Narratives

Next in the panorama of biblical accounts come the Canonical Gospels—Mark, Matthew, Luke, and John—together with Acts, which is volume two of Luke's depiction of the origin and initial expansion of early Christianity. Mark, the first to be written, can be pretty firmly dated to 70, some forty years after Jesus died and fifteen or twenty years after Paul's last letters. No doubt immediately triggered by Rome's catastrophic destruction of Jerusalem that ended the Jewish rebellion of 66 to 70, it set the chronological pattern for Matthew and Luke's accounts, traditionally dated c. 85, and hence the three are commonly termed the Synoptic Gospels because of their many parallels. John is thought to have been written between 90 and 100. Acts was long assigned a date close to that of Luke, but Richard Pervo's *Dating Acts* (2006, Polebridge Press) has led many objective scholars to accept a date of 110–120, and to wonder whether earlier and later versions of Luke may have existed.

From this we see that in all likelihood the canonical Christian texts were written during the hundred year period between 40 and 140—from Paul's early missions to the end of bar Kokhba's revolt (132–136). Accordingly, it is clear that Christianity grew up in an era riven by religious and political strife, and it can be no surprise that both numerous and diverse were the early communities devoted to the memory of Jesus. The existence of some two dozen entire or fragmentary gospels and a number of well-documented religious disagreements between early church leaders should prepare us for the fact that the five canonical accounts reflect many historical, theological and doctrinal divergences. They also do much to explain why the rapid and monolithic growth of Christianity depicted in Acts bears little resemblance to historical events.

To be a bit more specific, the players include not only the "Temple Jews" like the conservative Sadducees and the liberal Pharisees, but also the "Jesus Jews" of the Didache and those allied with Peter and James, as well as those who joined the Pauline 'heresy' and along with Gentile converts contributed to the growing movement that would soon become known as "Christianity." Beside these groups were the Coptic Christians of Egypt, the Gnostic communities reflected in the gospels of Thomas and Mary, and the followers of the much-maligned Marcion. This interesting fellow, a former shipmaster, came to believe that the God we meet in Genesis was not God, the father of Jesus; and in c. 144 he compiled what is often seen as the first New Testament—a volume consisting of Luke's gospel and ten of Paul's letters. He was, of course, soon declared a heretic.

These fractures, exacerbated by Roman oppression and inherent religious fanaticism, resulted in decades of infighting and recrimination among those claiming to represent the "correct" exposition of Jesus' message. Those who seek to understand the Christian scriptures must therefore come to recognize that myth and metaphor, fable and fantasy, dreams and dogmatism, will be constant companions as they progress along the path they hope will lead to spiritual serenity. And the numerous inventions and distortion of sources—along with variant readings and divergent translations of the extant texts—will provide an inexhaustible source of subject matter for discussions among scholars, theologians, Bible study groups, and families around holiday tables for many years to come.

Indeed, the problem of evangelical invention is so beset with booby-traps that one hardly knows how to address it. Where does one begin and how proceed? Following the order in which the books are printed would misrepresent the chronology of their writing and thus the way they are thematically related. Since they purport to relate the life and influence of Jesus, it would seem logical to begin with the well-known stories of his birth; but that would misrepresent the dates of authorship and thus the likely influence of one author on another. Therefore, I shall begin with a brief discussion of relevant aspects of Mark and John—probably the first and last of the canonical gospels—with some suggestions as to why they offer no birth narratives.

As for Mark, it is generally agreed that his gospel was so influenced by Titus' catastrophic sack of Jerusalem and the possibility of an apocalyptic end of the world—or at least of the present age—that only the emphatic proclamation of the arrival and inauguration of the promised Messiah (Mk 1:1–11) could take priority over an account of his birth. Besides, little would have been known about him except that he came from Nazareth (Mk 1:9; see also Jn 1:45–46). After all, he was one of the peasant class in Galilee, a people derogated by fellow Jews, to whom "Galilean" connoted "stupid" or "worthless"—much as "hillbilly" and "Okie" functioned in early twentieth-century America. One can reasonably suppose that he was yet to be so widely acclaimed that an important lineage would have been assigned to him. Also, it is generally accepted that Mark and those of his community were Gentiles (note the translation from Aramaic in 5:41), and thus would be unimpressed by a claim of Davidian ancestry.

Last of all, we must recognize that Mark was not a sophisticated narrator. His Greek is far from polished, and his syntax occasionally confused (see, e. g., 2:8–12a). And like the Jesus he portrays, he is impulsive and importunate: he often narrates in the present tense, and events occur at a rapid pace. One of his favorite words is *euthus*, rendered in English translations as "at once" and "immediately" (see, e.g., 2:8 and 12!). His Jesus repeatedly begins a statement with "look" or "listen"; and in 4:3 he doubles the command: "*Akouete, idou . . .* / Listen, look . . ." It's also worth noting that Mark's "Son of God" commonly refers to himself as "Son of Man" and usually has an urgent message to spread, a healing to perform, or a miracle to execute. He even likes to tell one story in between the beginning and end of another: see, e. g., 5:21–43. No subtle theologizing here, but two busy sons of Adam—author and subject—intent on their assigned tasks.

John, on the other hand, presents a Jesus whose feet never quite touch the ground because he is a divine being—the Logos (Word) who has existed from the beginning of time, was co-creator of the cosmos (1:1–3), and is the sole intermediary through which humans can be saved from the blight of sin and united with God. In fact, those who hear his words and believe in the One who sent him are already saved and will not face judgment (5:24). But the dual nature of this divine spirit—who "pitched his tent amongst us" (1:14) in order that God might choose some to be inspired by his presence—would remain as opaque to most as were the double meanings of his explanations to Nicodemus (3:1–12) and the woman at the well (4:7–15). Nevertheless, those who hear his words and believe in the One who sent him have already passed from death into life. To propose, then, that he was a product of the Galilean peasantry or that such a being could enter the world through the birth canal of a human female, would surely have been unthinkable.

So let's look at the extraordinary fictions of Matthew and Luke, both so familiar that we seldom think about them. First of all, the birth narratives are mutually contradictory in almost every major detail. They agree only on the names of the mother, father, and child—and of course the place of birth, which they both get wrong. Bethlehem was chosen because it was David's home turf, and the Messiah had to be of David's lineage. Political correctness commonly trumps fact in such cases.

We call these stories "gospels" and their authors "evangelists" because in Greek the genre is *euaggelion*, good news—in Old English *godspel*. Matthew, Mark, Luke and John are names assigned to anonymous scribes who wrote not history or biography, but proclamations intended to spread the word about the arrival of a new dispensation, a brighter future for humankind. We might even think of them as propagandists (with no negative connotation implied), for they were propagating a new way of understanding our relationship to God. And like all who are in the business of persuasion, each of them pitched his product to a particular audience. Thus it is no surprise that in the time of widespread chaos and terror that accompanied Rome's 'scorched earth' policy following the razing of Jerusalem in 70, Mark announced that the son of God had arrived (Mk 1:1, 11)—and what's more, he assigned to both Jesus (Mk 9:1) and obliquely to a Roman centurion (Mk 15:39) assurances that a new and better world was soon to come.

Some twenty years later Matthew and his community were less certain of a sudden change in world affairs, but they still held out hope for a brighter future. And we know that his audience was comprised largely of people brought up in the Jewish tradition, for early on he repeatedly cites the Hebrew Bible to show that Jesus' arrival was part of God's long-term plan of salvation. Unfortunately, his first four "oracles" (1:23 and 2:2, 15, 18) have no logical relation to the events they are said to authenticate, but first century literary protocols apparently permitted such "fudging." As for the fifth (2:23), scholars have yet to track it down. Matthew also calls in Persian astrologers to certify the ancient Jewish belief that one day the Gentile world would come to Israel for enlightenment, and invents the "slaughter of the innocents" to echo another popular legend about Pharaoh's similar attempt to kill Moses. He even sends the holy family off to Egypt so they can then retrace the Exodus before settling in Nazareth (remember, his Jesus was born at home in Bethlehem) and thus justify 1: 15—"Out of Egypt have I called my son." (The eponymous 'son' referred to in Hosea 11:1 was the Children of Israel.)

The details of this first-century narrative may not pass a twenty-first century sniff-test, but any contemporary Jew might well be attracted by its portrait of Jesus as a new and improved Moses.

Luke begins his tale by appealing to a very different cohort. To be sure, he pays proper respects to Jesus' roots by dating his account to the reign of the Jewish King of Judea (who as everyone knew ruled at the pleasure of a Roman governor) and by beginning the action with a Jewish priest of notable lineage and his wife who could claim Moses' brother as an ancestor. And he continues his carefully wrought prologue (like any sophisticated Greco-Roman he knows better than to introduce the main character before the stage is set) by establishing the wife as kinswoman of a virgin in Nazareth who was married to a descendant of David named Joseph. (It is all very neat and equally incredible; for members of the priestly caste of Judea would not have a teenage cousin married to a Galilean peasant.) And our author continues his brief bow to Judaism by assigning to Mary and Zechariah long and pious speeches assembled from quotes from the Hebrew Bible: the Jerusalem Bible lists twenty citations for the first and a dozen for the latter. Of course Zechariah's oration celebrates the coming birth of John the Baptist, but John is, after all, the master of ceremonies who serves as foil to enhance the more-than-human stature of his cousin; and virtues assigned to him can easily be associated with the one whom he has been sent to herald.

This becomes all the more telling when we learn that in 9 BCE "The Greeks of Asia" erected a stela in honor of Augustus, whom "Providence has sent as a savior for us and our descendants" inasmuch as "the birth-day of the god Augustus was the beginning of the glad tidings (*euag-galion*) for the world that resulted from him [and marked] the beginning of a new era." This monument, the Priene Stela (see *Wikipedia*) was surely well known in the late first century, and is widely regarded as a source of the Lukan text of the "Benedictus." And two verses later the next chapter begins by tying Jesus' birth to Augustus' reign, Quirinius' governorship, and the Roman tax that sent Joseph and Mary off to Bethlehem. Of course that detail is also a canard, for no Roman prefect would be sufficiently mad as to compel Galileans to travel to Judea to register for taxation—what, turn all those habitually rebellious peas-ants loose to roam the countryside? Or for that matter, what bureaucrat would know or care whether Joseph was a fourteenth generation descen-dant of David? But once again message trumps historicity, and Luke has deftly crafted the beginning of a tale that will present Jesus as a figure any reasonably sophisticated Gentile could recognize as a new and im-proved Caesar—one who represented an ancient religious tradition and who did not see war as the way to establish and maintain peace.

So much, then, for a cursory look at what the gospels tell us about Jesus' origins and what sort of underlying messages their authors might be offering us. Perhaps a brief examination of their accounts of his last days on earth will afford a few more useful insights on how to read and understand these ancient narratives.

First of all, we must acknowledge that the gospel accounts of the week before Jesus' execution and a few days after were written between forty and seventy years after the events they depict. That explains why Arthur Dewey's *Inventing the Passion* is so important; for it shows how Old Testament texts were thoroughly searched for passages that might be exploited to describe events that Jesus' followers could not have known of had they indeed occurred, but that would lend authoritative support to the evangelists' interpretations of their Lord's life, teachings, and significance. Why, for instance, did God allow such a good man to be so brutally killed? And what really happened to his body? What must we do to honor and perpetuate his memory? Given the shock, despair, and dashed hopes his followers surely experienced, and in view of their inability and that of the evangelists to discover what actually occurred, it is hardly surprising that the stories we have exhibit so many disagreements and discrepancies.

How else explain, for instance, the Gethsemane accounts in Mark and John? In the former, Jesus is so despondent that he asks why God has forsaken him; in the second, when he identifies himself to the arresting party of soldiers and police, they retreat and fall to the ground, whereupon Jesus orders them to release the disciples and willingly submits. How else conflate Mark's women who run screaming from the empty tomb with those of Matthew, who has them meet Jesus while returning from the tomb, or with the Lukan tale of a skeptical Mary Magdalen *et al.* and a curious Peter who went home amazed, and the Johannine scenario of Magdalen and Jesus in the garden, followed by a strange foot race between Peter and "the disciple Jesus loved" (guess who that was).

Or try to figure out why the original text of Mark has no post-resurrection appearances of Jesus, but Matthew has him meet the disciples on a mountain in Galilee. Luke, however, has him meet two disciples on the road to Emmaus and then magically appear to the eleven in Jerusalem. The Fourth Gospel offers both a meeting in Jerusalem and, in John 21, a later addition by a different writer, a reunion "fish-fry" in Galilee.

Now let us go on to other specific cases of authorial invention. It must be obvious to any critical reader that the evangelists created a good deal of their narrative material, an interesting example of which is the story of the empty tomb that derived from their misappropriation of Paul's report of Jesus' resurrection. For Paul, this phrase referred to a spiritual experience, not an historical event. This is clear from his definitive statement that "So it is with the resurrection of the dead. What is sown is perishable, what is raised is imperishable . . . it is sown a physical body, it is raised a spiritual body" (1 Cor 15:42–44)—and it is further certified by his report of multiple experiences by more than 500 people including himself (1 Cor 16:3–8). For his experience occurred years after Easter Sunday, at a time when Jesus had been long in his grave or long ago safely ensconced in Heaven. How can we make sense of that?

Brandon Scott has what seems to be the answer. In his magisterial *The Trouble with Resurrection*, Scott explains that Paul's "*ophthe Kepha*" (1 Cor 15:4)—traditionally mistranslated as "he was seen by Cephas" or "he appeared to Cephas"—should be rendered "he has been seen for the advantage of Cephas." Why? Because here as occasionally in the Greek New Testament and commonly in the Septuagint, the Greek translation of the Hebrew Bible, the "dative of advantage" is used to indicate an act of God, not a human action.[25] And no one knew better than Paul how advantageous it could be to claim to have been granted a special vision or audition.

But somewhere between Paul and Mark it must have become clear that a physical resurrection was necessary. Greco-Roman culture was so well provided with divine parents and ascending and descending deities that Paul's "spiritual body" either involved too great a paradox or offered too subtle a theological ontology. From that arose the necessity of depicting a resurrected—or rather resuscitated—Jesus. One solution appears in the non-canonical Gospel of Peter, where soldiers on guard at the tomb (lest the disciples steal Jesus' body and claim he was resurrected) saw the heavens open and two men approach the tomb. Thereupon, the stone magically rolled away, the two entered, and soon the guards saw them emerge supporting a third figure and followed by a cross. The heads of the two reached the clouds, and that of the third reached above the clouds and into the heavens. Then a voice from heaven said, "You have preached to those that sleep"; and the cross responded, "Yes."

That tale seems to have carried a good thing too far, but at least the tomb had provided a place from whence a lost body could reappear for long enough to be seen alive and even have a bite to eat to show those heretical Docetists that Jesus had truly risen from the dead and was not simply a divine hologram. And it might be further noted that Lloyd Geering, an internationally respected champion of the Christian tradition who this year celebrated his 103rd birthday, has persuasively argued that the original text of Mark ended with the Roman Centurion's confession (15:40) and the burial by Joseph and the empty tomb and all the rest reflect not one but two editorial additions.[26]

In recent years Luke's metanarrative has increasingly come to be seen as a two-volume historical novel—a label that has much to recommend it. His gospel traces the life of Jesus from beginnings in two little Judean and Galilean towns to his tragic death and glorious resurrection in the holy city of Jerusalem. Well, at the very end it does report one further event: "Then he led them out as far as Bethany, and, lifting up his hands, he blessed them. While he was blessing them, he withdrew from them and was carried up into heaven" (Luke 24:50–51). Alas, like many a fellow fictionalizer his flair for the dramatic finale led him to fumble. The text of the first volume may have been out of sight and out of mind

---

25. Scott, Bernard Brandon, *The Trouble with Resurrection*, pp. 107–113.
26. Geering, Lloyd, "Where Did St. Mark's Gospel End?", *The Fourth R*, May-June 2019.

when he began the sequel, in which he planned to show the seamless evolution of a small band of Jewish disciples in Jerusalem into a multi-ethnic throng of believers extending all the way to Rome, the capital city of a worldwide empire.

The trouble is that having sent the founder off to heaven, he tells us five verses later (Acts 1:3) that he remained with them for forty days, at which time ". . . he was lifted up and a cloud took him out of their sight" (1:9). And since a pair of angels who witnessed their puzzlement assured them that Jesus would reappear "in the same way as you saw him go" (1:11), one cannot but wonder whether yet more second comings are in store. To be sure, first-century narrative protocols were considerably less demanding in matters of precision and credibility than ours, but Lukan history loses some of its luster at this point. And even allowing for the flexible protocols of ancient historiography, the Pentecost story (Acts 2:1–11), with its dancing tongues of flame and Galilean tongues suddenly fluent in fifteen foreign languages, must be seen as fantasy and parsed symbolically rather than literally.

A subsequent tale further lowers our expectation of credible report-age. In Acts 5:1–11 we are told that a man and his wife who belonged to the early community sold a piece of land, broke a solemn vow by with-holding a portion of the proceeds, and lied about their perfidy. When separately confronted with their sins, both "fell down and died," where-upon "great fear seized all who heard of it." The clear implication is that God struck them down for their transgression. Shall we take that as part of Luke's concept of a loving God?

Two other episodes suggest that we approach his narratives with caution. Chapter 10 recounts the conversion of a Roman centurion, Cornelius, and his whole household, while Chapter 12 tells of the mi-raculous liberation of the apostle Peter, who lay in chains in Herod's prison awaiting execution. The first story is as believable as the second is impossible, but they share a serious flaw. Dennis Macdonald, one of Westar's most erudite scholars, has demonstrated that in all likelihood the story lines of these and two other passages in Acts were "borrowed" from Homer's classics.[27] Having been present at the presentation and discussion of his paper on Peter's escape, I can attest to his meticulous research and carefully wrought conclusions.

Of course one should not be surprised to discover that a first-cen-tury author borrowed from his predecessors and modified their work to hide the theft. In fact, to cite the works of Homer or Hesiod or echo them

---

27. MacDonald, Dennis R., *Does the New Testament Imitate Homer?*

almost to the point of plagiarism was an accepted way of gaining respect for one's own writings. The apocryphal text *The Wisdom of Solomon* is clearly a work of Hellenistic Judaism, which the Jerusalem Bible dates to "the middle of the first century B.C." (*sic*). And as relatively modern an author as Chaucer took pains to give the source of each of his tales—except for the two he made up, and which he credited to fictitious authors. Still, while recognizing that many truths have been communicated by works of fiction, it would seem a worthy habit to distinguish between factual accounts and fictitious—even (or especially?) from a pulpit.

For instance, shouldn't it be noted that Paul offers no details of his reported visionary experience near Damascus? He says only that ". . . when God called me . . . I went away at once into Arabia, and afterwards returned to Damascus" (Gal 1:15–17). That's it. No bright lights, no falling to the ground, no voice from heaven. Not only do those appear to be Lukan inventions (see Acts 9:3–8; 22:6–11; 26:13–19), but these three accounts don't tell the same story. Among other things, in the first case Luke writes the story in third person, but makes Jesus the narrator in the other two. And above all, it should be stressed that nowhere is a conversion mentioned. Like Jesus, Paul lived and died a Jew (Rom 11:1).

Even more problematic is the issue of Paul's collection, which involves both authors. According to Paul, it all began when he went to Jerusalem to obtain the *imprimatur* of the original Christian community led by James, Peter, and John. It is worth noting that he refers to them as "those who were supposed to be acknowledged leaders (what they actually were makes no difference to me; God shows no partiality)—those leaders contributed nothing to me" (Gal 1:6). It sounds like a less than convivial get-together. But Paul says he got what he wanted: their agreement that he would have a sort of exclusive franchise for the Gentile mission, while they would try to win Jews to what would become known as Christianity. All they asked in return, he says, is "that we remember the poor, which was actually what I was eager to do" (Gal 1:10). Aha, a bit of tit for tat to seal the agreement. But who really did the asking—or was it an offering? We'll never know, but I suspect that my old pal Gerd Lüdemann may not have been far from wrong in referring to it as "a polite bribe."[28] It was, after all, a Gentile world, and the blessing of the mother church would be worth a great deal in more ways than one.

In several of his letters Paul mentions the collection—exhorting his churches to put aside money, reminding them to have it ready when he

---

28. Lüdemann, Gerd. *Paul, the Founder of Christianity*, p. 42.

was coming on a visit—but his letters were pastoral in nature, not narrative. It was Luke who told about the final collection and delivery of the promised alms. Picking up his story upon their arrival at Tyre, we are told that the disciples there urged Paul not to go on to Jerusalem (Acts 21:4); and on arriving at Caesarea a prophet summoned from Judea issued an even stronger warning of impending danger. Whether these reflected local awareness of Paul's ill repute among 'the pillars' or Luke's literary foreshadowing is uncertain, but it could well be both. Then Luke tells us that upon their arrival in Jerusalem ". . . the brothers welcomed us warmly" (21:17), but when on the following day Paul was greeted by the assembled elders, they warned him that thousands of observant Jews had learned of his elimination of traditional practices and observances. (Not exactly a threat, but perhaps a polite threat?)

Strangely enough, the collection is never again mentioned, though the elders do suggest that to allay dangerous suspicions, Paul might do well to show good faith by absorbing the cost of purification rites for himself and four others who are "under a vow." (The nature of the vow is not specified, but a curious reader might recall that in 23:12 Luke tells of a plot in which more than forty loyal Jews swore an oath "neither to eat or drink until they had killed Paul". And sure enough, just as the purification rites are almost finished, someone cries out that Paul has taken a Gentile into the Temple with him. (One cannot help wondering whether Luke is creating a Jewish plot to get rid of him, or whether in fact he had been 'set up' after being "warmly welcomed".) Whatever the case, a riot ensues, and Paul is well battered before the Roman guard rescues him from a Jewish mob. One expects he would be charged with causing a riot, but it is the Jewish priesthood who press charges against him, apparently for heresy. Paul insists on his innocence, and more than two years pass while Roman officials and Jewish leaders drag out the case. At last, to avoid a trial in Jerusalem he appeals to the Emperor, and soon is on his way to Rome, where Luke says he lived under a kind of house arrest for two years, teaching about Jesus and preaching the message of the kingdom. He had taken the word of the Lord to Rome as he hoped; but just as Luke failed to tell what happened to the collection, he does not tell what finally happened to Paul. He may not have known, but it is more likely that he simply could not bear to describe his hero's execution.

Luke has indeed given us an epic tale, but we are left wondering not only how much of it we can believe, but also how much he may have left out. And we are also left suspecting that most of it was fiction calculated to persuade us that Christianity was a single ever-swelling stream that flowed from its source in Jerusalem to overspread the whole world. But in view of the many diverse communities that within two or three centuries had created strikingly different portraits of Jesus and worshipped him in many different ways, the Lukan metanarrative must also be seen as fiction. Nor did the process of diversification end, for in his monumental *Jesus Through the Centuries,* Jaroslav Pelikan shows us that every century or so Christianity has reimagined its risen Lord to conform with the contemporary worldview. Those who suppose that evolution applies only to biology are bound to misunderstand the fundamental nature of religion.

And finally, it should be noted that except for a brief epilogue (28:30) the Greek text ends with a single climactic word: *akousontai*— "they will listen." Paul, having soundly chastised the Jewish leaders of the Roman community for their failure to accept his "good news of salvation", assures them that the Gentiles will welcome his gospel—and thereby take their place as God's chosen people. Can it be that Luke has placed on Paul's lips the first clear declaration of Christian supersessionism, and the beginning of what came to full flower in the Holocaust?

So much for examples of the evangelists' inventions; let us now consider a few cases of their modification of sources. Editing the work of others provided a useful way for New Testament authors to flavor, slant, or even distort earlier accounts. To be sure, the Synoptics—Mark, Matthew, and Luke—have so many closely parallel passages that most scholars, accepting Mark's priority (c. 70 CE), agree that Matthew and Luke (c. 85–90) have relied heavily on the earlier text in telling the story of Jesus. A good example can be seen by comparing three versions of a familiar pericope:[29]

Mark 2:16–17	Matt 9:11–12	Luke 5:30–31
And whenever the Pharisees' scholars saw him eating with sinners and toll collectors, they would question his disciples: "What's he doing eating with toll collectors?" When Jesus overhears, he says to them:" "Since when do the able-bodied need a doctor? It's the sick who do."	And whenever the Pharisees saw this, they would question his disciples: "Why does your teacher eat with toll collectors and sinners?" When Jesus overheard, he said, "Since when do the able-bodied need a doctor? It's the sick who do."	And the Pharisees and their scholars would complain to his disciples: "Why do you people eat and drink with toll collectors and sinners?" In response, Jesus said to them: "Since when do the healthy need a doctor? It's the sick who do."

29. These and subsequent citations in this section use the Scholars' Version translation. See Funk and Hoover, *The Five Gospels*: pp. 12–13.

And we find what must seem a plagiaristic correspondence between two passages in Matthew and Luke:

Matt 3:7–10	Luke 3:7–9
When he saw that many of the Pharisees and Sadducees were coming for baptism, (John) said to them, "You spawn of Satan! Who warned you to flee from the impending doom? Well then, start producing fruit suitable for a change of heart, and don't even *think* of saying to yourselves, 'We have Abraham as our father.' Let me tell you, God can raise up children for Abraham right out of these rocks. Even now the axe is aimed at the root of the trees. So every tree not producing choice fruit gets cut down and tossed into the fire."	So (John) would say to the crowds, "You spawn of Satan! Who warned you to flee from the impending doom? Well then, start producing fruit suitable for a change of heart, and don't even *start* saying to yourselves, 'We have Abraham for our father.' Let me tell you, God can raise up children for Abraham right out of these rocks. Even now the axe is aimed at the root of the trees. So every tree not producing choice fruit gets cut down and tossed into the fire."

But in this case, no Markan parallel exists. Clearly another source is indicated, and for such close correspondence, it must have been a written text, because oral transmission would not have been so precise. Besides, about two hundred verses fall into this category. Scholarly attempts to explain such striking agreements began in 1801, and by 1838 had progressed to assigning the material a name: the Sayings Source, or Q—from *Quelle*, the German for "source."

In recent years, John Kloppenborg has defined a document that was begun as early as the forties and evolved in three stages, and William Arnal has tentatively identified its archivists as Galilean municipal scribes who worked for Roman administrators but were moved by the prophetic teachings of a fellow Jew who yearned for a new dispensation. One striking example of how Matthew and Luke put different "spins" on a Q text is their different renderings of the Lord's Prayer:

Matt 6:9–13	Luke 11:2–4
Our Father in the heavens Your name be revered. Impose your divine domain, Enact your will on earth as you have in heaven, Provide us with the bread we need for the day. Forgive us our debts to the extent that we have forgiven those in debt to us. And please don't subject us to test after test, But rescue us from the evil one.	**Father,** your name be revered. Impose your divine domain. Provide us with the bread we need day by day. Forgive our sins, since we too forgive everyone in debt to us. And please don't subject us to test after test.

The Seminar scholars further concluded that the original from which Matthew and Luke took their texts probably read much like this:

Q
Father,
Your name be revered,
Impose your divine domain,
Provide us with the bread we need for the day,
Forgive us our debts to the extent we have forgiven those in debt to us.

From all this, three things may be observed: First, modern versions of this famous prayer have undergone a considerable evolution—one especially noteworthy addition being Protestantism's adoption of a doxology based on 1 Chronicles 29:11. Second, the traditional bromide that claims inerrancy for the Bible deserves to be summarily rejected. Third, and most important for our present purpose, is the scholarly consensus that when Matthew and Luke exhibit different performances of Q, Luke generally follows the original more closely.

One of the best examples of this is the highly revered passage known as the Beatitudes (Matt 5:3–11). It is the first part of the familiar Sermon on the Mount, so called because Matthew tells us that Jesus climbed a hill in order to address a large crowd of followers. (He may also have been suggesting a parallel to Moses receiving the Law on Mount Sinai.)

The version of the text I memorized in Sunday School (Matt 5:1–12) contains a list of nine situations that mark a person as "blessed." This term is problematic, for the Greek original is *makarioi*, derived from *makar*—happy, lucky, especially favored. The Scholar's Version (SV) uses "Congratulations"; and with slight contextual changes the word could be rendered "Fortunate" or even "Rejoice."

In any case, Matthew has apparently edited Q very freely. He and Luke concur that those who grieve will be consoled and the persecuted will be rewarded; but Matthew changes "the poor" (read 'destitute') to "the poor in spirit" (whatever that means) and "the hungry" to "those who hunger and thirst for justice." And the remaining blessings, borrowed from the Greek version of the Hebrew Bible, promise rewards for virtue rather than relief from distress.

In Luke 6:17–26, however, we read that after a night of prayer on a mountain (a typically Lukan theme) Jesus came down to a level place (hence "The Sermon on the Plain") and offered a large gathering of his followers four of the blessings found in Matthew together with four curses: the latter for those who are rich, well-fed, happy, and well-regarded. Given these quite different performances of Q, one might

47

reasonably infer that Matthew's community included one or more wealthy persons, a number of sensitive souls in need of spiritual reassurance, and some who would be alienated by blunt reality. No wonder that Luke's sermon remains all but unknown.

A brief postscript is in order. In addition to crediting Q, the Westar scholars list the Gospel of Thomas not simply as a parallel but as a source for the verses on the poor, the hungry, and the persecuted. And as we shall see in a later section, several parables—some from Q and some found only in Luke—have versions in Thomas that lack the allegorical elements found in the canonical texts. This suggests that they were earlier and therefore likely sources—in other words, that portions of the Bible may have come back along the Silk Road from Edessa, the probable home of the Thomas community. Like Q, early editions of this long-lost document may date to c. 50 CE, and thus precede Mark by two decades and Matthew and Luke by three or four; but its lack of conformance with evolving Christian doctrine rendered it heretical. If a hidden copy had not been discovered in 1945 at Nag Hammadi, Egypt, important insights into the development of gospel literature might have been lost forever, and the powerful influence of Greek Platonism on Christianity never fully recognized.

Another provocative case of editing sources is that found in the several accounts of Jesus' baptism. Mark exhibits no hesitation in assuring us that John baptized him in the Jordan, whereupon a voice from heaven pronounced him the Son of God. But by the time Matthew was writing his gospel it had occurred to many of a growing number of the faithful that the divine savior had no need to be cleansed of sin. As *The Five Gospels* puts it, the story was "an embarrassment to the Christian community that wanted to distance itself from both the Baptist movement and rabbinic Judaism." To avoid this, Matthew has John demur at performing the cleansing rite, and lets Jesus overrule him by observing that participating in common religious practices could hardly be objectionable. Luke sees the problem too, and tries to have it both ways: he does not say that John baptized Jesus, but that he was imprisoned by Herod "after all the people had been baptized" and that after Jesus "had been baptized" the voice from heaven did its duty. Predictably, the Fourth Gospel avoids any mention of Jesus being baptized; the author finds it more important to emphasize the contrast between John's baptism with water and Jesus' promised baptism of the Holy Spirit, and to have John testify that he saw the spirit descend on Jesus, heard the voice from heaven, and "that this is the Son of God." Apparently the Evangelist declined to picture a mere mortal fine-tuning the son of God.

Immediately following the baptism accounts, the Synoptic authors offer yet another example of source management. Mark no doubt derives from an oral source his report of Jesus' being tested by Satan. (What better evidence of his divinity than the ability to overcome any and all temptations?) But Mark says only that "the Spirit immediately drove him out into the wilderness" and that when his forty-day ordeal was over, "the angels waited on him." Not a word about the nature of the tests or how he had managed to pass them. Once again it is Q to the rescue, with a detailed script of the dialogue. Since only Jesus and Satan were present, the account of their discourse is legendary and comes from the Q author, who has drawn on the Hebrew Bible for the three lessons imparted. And in this case Matthew and Luke offer almost verbatim reports, but reverse the order of temptations two and three. Matthew moves the scene vertically, from the wilderness to the spire of the Temple to the top of a mountain; Luke goes from the desert to a mountain top to the pinnacle of the Temple. Has Luke created a miniature of Jesus' career path from baptism in the Judean wilderness to death in Jerusalem, or does he mean to imply that not putting God to the test is a demand of greater importance than exclusive reverence? Or both? Or neither?

Clearly, the discussion of manipulated sources has focused largely on Matthew, Luke, and to a lesser degree Mark, whose gospel must have been based largely on second- and third-hand oral traditions as well as passages from the Hebrew Bible—a source that Jesus' earliest followers presupposed to foretell or explain events and aspects of his life, his tragic death, and his enduring importance. And for the most part John's sources are difficult to determine, for his narrative frame contradicts that of the Synoptics in nearly every particular. It has been observed that whereas the first three gospels at least seem to be biographical in form (though Richard Pervo's terms "apologetic historiography" and "legitimating narrative" are surely more precise), John presents us with a spiritual drama the verisimilitude of which is often lost in lengthy arias beginning with "I am . . ."[30]

To be sure we find hints of other source material: scholars agree that that some of John's pericopes reflect a collection of miracle stories known as "The Signs Source"; and the story of the woman taken in adultery (7:53–8:11) is missing in the earliest manuscripts, but sometimes appears after 7:36, 21:25, or Luke 21:38.[31] And only John has the Last Supper occur on the correct date for a Seder. Besides, his account

---

30. See *The Five Gospels*, p. 419.
31. See the footnote in NRSV.

of the expulsion of the money changers, while oddly placed in Chapter 2, closely follows the synoptic versions, where the incident is set in Holy Week. Last but not least, one might reasonably propose that John's primary source is to be found in Exodus 3:14: "I am who I am"—a central theme on which he rings seven lengthy changes beginning on 6:35, 8:12, 8:58, 10:11, 11:25, 14:6, and 15:1.

Of Forces and Sources

The time has now come to take note of two further explanations for the existence of conflict and even contradiction in biblical texts. The first is the power of deeply rooted hopes and expectations. Oppressed by a confiscatory Roman occupation and a corrupt Temple cult, the people of the Jewish homeland were understandably susceptible to apocalyptic beliefs. Some sort of messianic deliverance, even if it required an intervening catastrophe, was always in the air. And early followers of Jesus added to familiar Jewish apocalyptic scenarios the conviction that a just and loving God could not simply overlook the cruel and summary execution of his divine son, but must hasten to put an end to the sociopolitical system that not only permitted but brought about this existential tragedy. We see this in Paul's preaching that the end was near—not the end of the world, as many have been led to assume, but the end of a corrupt era and its replacement with a more humane dispensation. (The usual term for that eventuality was "the kingdom of God"; but probably a better one would be "God's reign"—which I take to involve a universal commitment to living up to the moral ideal of love of neighbor.)

In its primitive form (see 1 Thess 4:15) this promised that Jesus would soon return and carry the faithful off to live with him in heaven. Some years later we find a more measured assurance of salvation: ". . . for the present form of this world is passing away" (1 Cor 7:31). Some fifteen years later, the earliest gospel repeats this refrain when Mark has Jesus tell his disciples that ". . . some standing here . . . will not taste death until . . . the kingdom of God has come . . ." (Mark 9.1).

But shortly before those words were written, history intervened. In the late sixties political instability in the Empire led Jewish Zealots to mistake indecision for weakness, and they launched an all-out effort to drive the hated Romans from Jerusalem. They did not represent a new phenomenon, for when Jesus was a boy, an uprising in Galilee ended with thousands of rebels crucified along the highways. And in the Jerusalem he knew, sicarii—"dagger-men"—ambushed Roman soldiers whom they left bleeding to death in back alleys. Two further details are worth noting: First, Mark 15:7 and Luke 23:19 describe Barabbas (Hebrew for Son of the Father!) as one charged with insurrection and murder. Second, in the Greek original of Mark 15:27 and Matt 27:38, the two "thieves" crucified with Jesus were called *lestes*, a word that can credibly be rendered "revolutionary"[32] or "terrorist."

---

32. *The New Greek-English Interlinear New Testament*, p. 396, John 18:40.

The Zealot rebellion was crushed in 70: thousands were killed, thousands fled, the city was sacked, the Temple destroyed, and sporadic fighting went on until the defeat of Masada in 73. Now bereft of its Temple, Judaism was reinstituted under Pharisaic leadership, and surprising as it may seem, Jewish life went on much as before. But relations between the early Church and the Synagogue deteriorated: Gentile God-fearers and Christians felt little love for those who had brought about the catastrophe. And by the time the later gospels were being written it no longer appeared that civilization—or even the present era—was about to end. Life went on, and Christians and Jews alike had to re-imagine their present situation, their future, and their theology.

Zealot resistance went on until Simon bar Kokhba's defeat in 136; that event and the contemporaneous beginnings of Pharisaic Judaism are often taken to mark the time when Christianity and Judaism finally became distinct traditions. But the parting had dragged out over half a century of often bitter rivalry, and any who seek to appreciate the effects of that conflict on the gospel texts would do well to read James Carroll's exposition in *Christ Actually: Reimagining Faith in the Modern Age*. The anti-Judaism that began with Mark grew with Matthew's animus toward traditional Jews, intensified with John's repetitious disparagement of "the Jews," and found its climax in Luke's reassignment of divine favor.[33] It constitutes an indelible stain on the record of Christianity—one that continues even to this day.

In short,

So it was that historical forces
Led apostles to edit their sources;
And thereby to stray
From Jesus' Way[34]
In reporting his deeds and discourses.

---

33. Acts 28:28.
34. An early name for Christianity was "The Way."

Biblical Narratives
A Conclusion

Surely traditional Christians will be profoundly challenged by Rex Hunt's exposition of Religious Naturalism, in which he cites former fundamentalist Michael Dowd's *cri de coeur* entitled *Thank God for Evolution*:

> Tell me a creation story more wondrous than that of a living cell forged from the residue of exploding stars. Tell me a story of transformation more magical than that of a fish hauling out onto land and becoming amphibian, or a reptile taking to the air and becoming bird, or a mammal slipping back into the sea and becoming whale. Surely this science-based culture of all cultures can find meaning and cause for celebration in its very own cosmic creation story.[35]

And what strict literalist dare dismiss the closing warning of Douglas L. Griffin's "Reading the Bible as Theological Fiction":

> It could be that in our age, those secular voices most vilified as opposing the Christian faith are actually the ones closest to the Epiphany witness of the magi. The divide between the secular and sacred, Epiphany and Enlightenment, is an unnatural divide. It simply does not have to be that way. Sacred and secular are not opposites. They are complementary. Reading the Bible as theological fiction can free us from slavery to facts and traditions and unleash our imaginations to behold horizons of meaning heretofore not recognized but waiting to come to light.[36]

As Lloyd Geering, former Old Testament professor and Principal of the Presbyterian Seminary of New Zealand has warned,[37] the book of Ecclesiastes gravely undermines any literal acceptance of the rest of the rest of the Hebrew Bible; and even those who ignore the many discrepancies of the canonical gospels cannot deny that the letter of James constitutes a direct attack on Paul's central doctrine of salvation by faith alone.

It's time to come clean about the nature of the fictions that have long been used to define our faith. The eminent theologian Rudolf Bultmann

---

35. *The Fourth R*, November-December 2020, p.4.
36. *The Fourth R*, January-February 2020 p. 20.
37. Geering, *Such Is Life*, pp. 9–10.

described the issue concisely: the biblical authors lived in a three-story universe of heaven, earth, and the underworld—a tripartite world that was ruled by supernatural forces and beings. We today, however, inhabit a vast but seamless universe, the origin and extent of which remain a mystery, but all aspects of which are governed by a single code of natural law. The ancients could no more imagine the world we know than we can accept the reality of theirs. We could no more expect Jesus or Paul to understand a trip in a Boeing 747 as anything less than a divine miracle than we should be willing to accept the possibility of divine suspension of the laws of physics.

In his brilliant essay "Scripture, God-talk and Jesus" my old pal Nigel Leaves—alas, no longer with us—cited Benjamin Jowett, who in 1860 insisted that the Bible "is to be interpreted like other books, with attention to the character of is authors and the prevailing state of civilization and knowledge, with allowance for peculiarities in style and language, and modes of thought and figure of speech."[38] Nigel went on to say, "Today we must broaden that advice by undertaking a critical examination of the theological biases of its writers and the reasons for their particular understandings of God. This is not to denigrate their search for the divine, but to read the texts with eyes wide open to the historical, social, and cultural factors that influenced them."[39]

This caveat will prove especially pertinent in examining the final genre of biblical fiction that I shall discuss—the parables of Jesus; for we have for too long read his sometimes cryptic narratives without taking the trouble to consider factors that shaped the worldview of his first-century Jewish audience. And as we shall see, that failure has often distorted our understanding of the message of the poetic genius whom Thomas Jefferson described as the greatest moral teacher of humankind.

---

38. Jenks, Gregory, ed., *The Once and Future Scriptures*, p. 76.
39. Ibid., pp. 76–77.

Parables

The word "parable" is a transliteration of the Greek *parabolē*, which means "to throw or place alongside of," and thus indicates a metaphoric comparison. The Greek in turn translates the Hebrew *mashal* (to be like), a word that can refer to a riddle, a proverb, or a wise saying, and thus denotes a broad genre of which parables are a sub-category. Brandon Scott defines parable as "a mashal that employs a short narrative fiction to reference a transcendental symbol," and further observes: "in rabbinic parables [that symbol] is the Torah; in Jesus' parables it is the Kingdom of God." That is why so many of Jesus' stories begin "The kingdom of God is like . . ."[40] Yet it cannot be too strongly emphasized that the metaphors employed involve elements of everyday human life, not theological or moral abstractions. And being "of the earth, earthy," the comparisons they invoke vary from imprecise to arcane. In short, one should no more attempt to assign a simple moral to a parable than to render in clear prose the "meaning" of a fine poem. To be sure, some seem pretty easy to understand; but the very first parable in a New Testament text raises serious questions.

The Sower (Mk 4:3–8)

This parable likens a farmer sowing seed to a missionary spreading the good news of the kingdom: where the soil is poor the harvest will be poor, where fertile, it will be abundant. But apparently Mark's community didn't do metaphors very well or the folks thereabout may have been hostile and hard-hearted, for he has Jesus decide to translate the message. The puzzling result is that in vv. 13–20 the differing soils become different kinds of people:

> [14]The sower sows the seed. [15]These are the ones on the path where the word is sown; when they hear the word . . . [20]And these are the ones sown on the good soil . . .

Apparently Mark's main point is that not everyone who hears Jesus' message will accept it and pass it on to others, but a few will be inspired and grow in the faith and provide the kingdom with a rich harvest of souls. But another agenda appears in vv. 10–12: Mark has Jesus say that he preaches in parables so that unbelievers will not understand and thus never be worthy of salvation. Let the reader be wary!

---

40. Scott, Brandon, *Hear Then the Parable*, p. 8.

Rating authenticity: a brief excursus

The Five Gospels, a 1993 publication by Robert Funk, Roy Hoover and the Jesus Seminar, was the report of an investigation by more than 100 highly qualified biblical scholars and clergy. Their goal was to assess the authenticity of sayings attributed to Jesus in the four canonical gospels and the Gospel of Thomas, a text unknown for some fifteen centuries until its discovery in 1945. After eight years of study and debate they voted with colored beads on the accuracy of each passage that the authors had placed on Jesus' lips:

Red—Jesus said something very much like this.
Pink—Jesus probably said something rather like this.
Gray—Jesus didn't say this, but it represents ideas similar to this.
Black—Jesus didn't say this; it represents a later tradition.

The beads were assigned a numerical value from 3 to 0, and the weighted average for each saying or portion thereof was assigned a numerical rating and the text printed in color: 0 to .25, black; .26 to .50, gray; .51 to .75, pink; .76 to 1.0, red. Mk 4:3–8 was rated .54, pink, and vv. 13–20 were printed in black.

The Leaven (Matt 13:33 / Luke 13:20–21) .83, Red; (Thom 96:1–2) .56, Pink.

"One day a housewife kneaded some leaven into three measures of flour until the two were thoroughly blended. That's an appropriate metaphor for what the Kingdom of God will be like." (my rendering)

But one of his listeners might have objected: "Wait a minute; leaven is one of the most powerful symbols of religious impurity,[41] but at three important junctures of Israel's history that specific amount of meal indicates the divine presence.[42] Are you telling us that in God's kingdom the secular and the sacred are one and the same?"

"Yep."

The Leaven received the Jesus Seminar's highest rating for authenticity of all the parables. This will not be a great surprise to those who are aware that a number of other traditions—e. g. Islam, Buddhism, Taoism, and Zoroastrianism—lend doctrinal support to the indivisibility of our secular and spiritual lives. Its secure place in the Christian

---

41. See, e.g. Exod 12:14–15; Matt 16:11–12; 1 Cor 5:6–7a.
42. Gen 18:1–6; Jdg 6:19; 1 Sam 1:24.

tradition is further attested by Col 3:23, and beautifully expressed in George Herbert's famous hymn (c. 1650), which begins, "Teach Me, My God and King/ In all things Thee to see/ And what I do in anything/ To do it as for Thee."

Two other points should be noted: First, three measures of flour (an ephah) is about a bushel, enough to make bread for a small village. Second, although the Gospel of Thomas usually preserves parables in a more original and therefore more authentic form, this version of the story omits the crucial three measures of meal and has the woman use a little leaven and make the dough into large loaves. The contrast between small and large is a repeated theme of this author; and this and other variations result in a .65 rating (pink) as opposed to the .83 rating (red) assigned to Matthew and Mark's nearly verbatim texts.

The Good Samaritan (Luke 10:30–35) .81, Red

"One day on the lonely and dangerous road from Jerusalem down to Jericho thieves mugged a defenseless traveler, stripped him of all possessions, and left him lying by the wayside, half alive and naked.[43] Before long both a Temple priest and a Levite bound for their month of R&R in cool, green Jericho hastened on their way paying him no heed.[44] Then along came a Samaritan,[45] who not only cleaned and bound his wounds, but carried him to an inn and paid for his recovery time."[46] (my rendering)

Bob Funk and Brandon Scott were among the first to recognize Luke's contextualization of Jesus' parable, a strategy that changed it into a chreia, an example or pronouncement story—i.e., one used to introduce an important teaching. Mark, Matthew, and Luke introduce six similar stories by having someone approach Jesus and ask him a question about faith or doctrine. In Mk 12:28 and Mt 22:34 it is, "What is the greatest

---

43. For Jesus' listeners the man's nakedness would not only connote utter shame and desperation, but also afford none of the then common indications of class, status, ethnicity, or religious affiliation.

44. Because Temple officials had close fiscal and political ties with the Roman governor and demanded what for the poor were exorbitant fees to conduct necessary rites, its functionaries were widely resented by the peasantry.

45. Following the Assyrian conquest and repopulation of Samaria in 721 BCE, Jews and Samaritans had been bitter enemies.

46. The mere touch of a Samaritan rendered a Jew ritually unclean; to be beholden to one would be a source of great personal shame.

commandment?" The issue in Mk 10:17, Mt 19:17, and Lk 18:18 is "What must I do to have eternal life?" But Luke uses this opening a second time in 10:25—presumably because his Gentile audience would not understand "the greatest commandment," a common doctrinal debate issue among Jews. And instead of having Jesus answer the question, Luke has him hand it back to the questioner, a Torah scholar, who in vv. 26–28 gives the correct answer, but follows it by asking Jesus to define "neighbor" (v. 29).

Then, when the parable ends, (v. 35) Luke completes the context (vv. 36–37) by having Jesus call on the scholar to answer his own question, which again he does correctly. Luke thus turns the whole narrative into an example story—that is, one depicting a course of moral behavior one should imitate.

In short, Jesus' listeners did not hear the introduction/conclusion frame, but only the parable, which must have been quite a shock to them. No doubt they were expecting a fellow Jew to come along and tend to the victim; for just as many stories today begin with "A minister, a priest, and a rabbi . . .," a common first-century formula was "A priest, a Levite and an Israelite. . . ." But in this case, alas, the expected rescuer is one of those detested Samaritans. How could one good Jew expect another to respect and even be grateful to someone they all had been brought up to hate and despise?

Like it or not, Jesus was not urging his listeners to be what we now call a "good Samaritan"; he was saying that every Samaritan is your neighbor, for we have one common father; and to establish God's kingdom on earth you'd better start behaving accordingly!

As with the idea that the sacred and secular are one, this was a radical teaching, and one we still observe more in the breach than in the observance. Parables are not Sunday school lessons with a nice little moral attached, but challenges to change our lives.

The Prodigal Son (Luke 15:11–32) .70, Pink

As was true in the two preceding cases, the implicit message of this parable is not readily apparent to many readers. Most of us know the broad outline of the story, but being unfamiliar with the first-century world we cannot imagine why Brandon Scott would call it "The Prodigals." The reason is that he sees the father as equally prodigal, if not more so. No proper Palestinian patriarch of that time would dream of dividing his patrimony. In fact, as the ruler of his little kingdom he would take his son's impetuous request as tantamount to a wish for his father's death. Instead, Dad swallows his pride, hands over the money, and thus calls down shame on the entire family.[47] Jesus' listeners would have been aghast.

The son is equally shameless, for he fritters away the entire sum on wine, women, and song. Worse yet, as we subsequently learn (v. 30), the family—and no doubt the neighbors—all hear of his perfidy; the "faraway country" (v. 13) was not all that far away. Soon the miserable wretch is reduced to feeding pigs for Gentile farmers—the lowest possible occupation for a well-born Jewish lad—and decides to go home with his tail between his legs and beg to be a family servant. Then we learn, perhaps to our surprise, that his father has been sitting by the window, peering down the road, hoping against hope for his son's return. Is that how a proud proprietor is likely to behave towards a renegade child? And it gets worse, for upon seeing the lad's approach, he loses all patriarchal dignity and runs to greet him. To do so, of course, he had to hoist the hem of his robe well above his knees and display his bare legs. Even Jesus' peasant listeners would have found that combination of inelegant behaviors shocking.

Then, to add to his display of self-abandon, he threw his arms around the wastrel and kissed him. (Note: according to Luke it was not a *phileo* kiss—"to greet or welcome," but one of the *kataphileo* variety—"to kiss tenderly, to caress.") It gets still worse, for Dad refuses to hear Son's apology. Instead, he gives orders that his own best robe and sandals and signet ring—all symbols of authority—be given to the revenant, and that a celebratory feast is in order: after all, he says, "My son was dead, and has come back to life . . ."

But there suddenly arises a complication (one that may or may not have been part of the original parable). An older son who is hard at work in the fields hears the commotion, learns of its cause, and is outraged at the display of favoritism. He accuses his father of unfair treatment and refuses to join the party. Again, the patriarch plays the pussycat; addressing his adult son as "my child," he repeats his earlier dictum: We have to celebrate, he says, ". . . because this brother of yours was dead and has come back to life . . ."

As Scott observes, everything the father does is contrary to the canons of male behavior in an honor-shame society, but instead conforms to what any mother would likely do. Therefore, if like other parables this tale is to be understood as somehow symbolic of God's kingdom, the

---

47. For such insights into first-century social mores, see Scott, pp. 108–122.

'take-away' seems clear: When and if the kingdom comes, it will be run by mother's rules.

The Evil Tenants/ The Leased Vineyard (Thom 65;1–7) .61, Pink; (Mark 12:1–8; Matt 21:33–39; Luke 20:9–15a) all .27, Gray.

This parable is probably the paradigm case of evangelists adding details to a story in order to create, or at least strongly imply, 'a moral of the story' that was not originally intended. Thomas' version, despite an ambiguity at the very beginning, is probably very close to Jesus' original; and Thom 66 (rated black) must have been an early addition. It likely represents the first step in the process of allegorization since the synoptic authors made it part of the performance.

> 65.A [moneylender / good man] who owned a vineyard leased it to some farmers in return for a share of the proceeds. But when he sent his slave to collect the agreed portion, they beat him almost to death. On hearing this, his master said "Perhaps they didn't recognize him," and sent another slave. They beat that one as well. Then the master sent his son and said, "Maybe they'll show him some respect." But knowing he was heir to the property, they grabbed him and killed him. Anyone here with two good ears had better listen! 66.Jesus said, "Show me the stone that the builders rejected: that is the keystone."

Obviously, a key issue is whether a lacuna in the Coptic manuscript should be reconstructed to indicate a good man or a usurer. Kind-hearted moneylenders were not often to be found in Jesus' world, and Thomas is wont to condemn business dealings of any sort: "Buyers and merchants [will] not enter the places of my Father" (Thom 64:12.) Furthermore, it is difficult to imagine a good man sending his son on an errand that got two slaves almost killed. What part of "No" did this good man fail to understand? He seems to be so concerned with an assault on his honor (and the loss of profit) that he is willing to risk his own son's life to repair the damage. To be sure, the questionable logic of the farmers' assumption that the death of the heir would secure their title to the vineyard is not convincing; but first-century Galilee was a rather lawless place, and the master gave little indication of using any kind of force to back his demands.

On the basis of Thomas 65 alone, then, what could Jesus' point have been? Perhaps that when you live in a "wild west" world, you had better rely on the sheriff or a judge to deal with dangerous challenges? Certainly a usurer would know how to protect his interests unless he was incredibly foolish, prideful, and inconsiderate of others. And in that case, how could he be called "good"? Maybe Jesus was issuing a warning like that made famous by the Sergeant in Hill Street Blues: "Let's be careful out there!" And that would be especially appropriate for a time and place characterized by confiscatory economic programs in both the political and ecclesiastical arenas and lacking in organized local law enforcement.

So where did Thomas 66 come from? It would seem likely that someone searching for a scriptural precedent to bolster an interpretation saw the word "son," thought of Jesus who had died bearing a message from his father, and recalled a psalm that promised God's deliverance:

> This is the gate of the Lord; the righteous shall enter through it.
> I thank you that you have answered me and have become my salvation.
> The stone that the builders rejected has become the chief cornerstone. (Ps 118:20–22)

Then someone recalled Isaiah 5:1–7 (check it out!), and soon Mark had Jesus doing allegory: the vineyard owner is God, the rebellious tenants are Israel, and the mistreated servants are the prophets. Matthew, the Jewish evangelist who remembered that Golgotha was outside the walls of Jerusalem, allows Jesus to predict future events by having the malefactors drag the son out of the vineyard before killing him. And all three of the synoptic iterations make it clear that God would find new beneficiaries for his covenant. No wonder this was a favorite story among early Christians!

The Dishonest Steward / The Shrewd Manager
(Luke 16:1–8a) .77, Red.

Not only has this parable baffled exegetes for centuries, but Luke himself seems to have been puzzled by it. His fumbling attempts to explain what it means (vv. 8b–13) cannot be taken seriously. As the notable parable scholar C. H. Dodd put it, they might be seen as a list of sermon topics, but do nothing to deal with the difficult fact that Jesus seems to approve of a carefully planned double theft.

Early on I took two hints from Chaucer that allowed me to imagine I had a solution to the problem. In the course of a decade or two I tried it out in several sermons, and ended up with an analysis that appeared in *The Fourth R* of November/December 2013. Now you can try it out— and remember that although it does not appear in the text, the final line is "What do **you** think?"

The Magnanimous Master

The parable variously referred to as "the Unjust Steward," "The Crafty Servant," or "The Shrewd Manager" is an intriguing one. A couple of parallels from an author I particularly revered in my years as an English teacher came to mind as I read of the steward's fall from grace and his desperate attempts at damage control. Then a minister friend told me it is a passage commonly avoided by preachers. The prominent German scholar Gunther Bornkamm explains their reluctance: since it contains "not a word of moral indignation . . . the average pious reader . . . gives this parable a wide berth."[48] Naturally, this was sufficient reason for a brash neophyte to include the parable in a series of sermons dealing with Jesus' narrative teachings. The lack of agreement among commentators soon explained the widespread reluctance to go wading in this hermeneutical bog. Indeed, the discussion in *Peake's Commentary* began with the warning, "This is the most difficult of all parables, and no interpretation is wholly satisfactory."[49] And yet *The Five Gospels* colors it red, rating it close to "Leaven" and "The Samaritan" in authenticity.[50] As I said, it is intriguing.

I soon enough discovered a strong consensus that Luke 16:1–15 contains a core parable with several appended comments either assembled or created by the author, and that the intent of the added logia in verses 8b-15 was to absorb some of the shock of verse 8a: "The master praised the dishonest steward for his astuteness" (JB) or "The master praised the dishonest manager because he had acted shrewdly" (SV). Some found the commendation of theft especially jarring since "master" translates *kyrios*, the same word commonly used as a title for Jesus. Then, just as one is ready to see verses 1–8a as the parable and 8b–15 as notes for three separate sermons,[51] along comes Dom Crossan with the argument that verse 8a cannot be authentic because it is logically inconsistent with verses 1–2,

There was this rich man whose manager had been accused of squandering his master's property. He called him in and said,

48. Bornkamm, Gunther, *Jesus of Nazareth*. New York: Harper & Row, 1975, p. 88.

49. Black, Matthew (ed.), *Peake's Commentary on the Bible*. Nashville: Thomas Nelson Publishers, 1987, p. 863.

50. Funk, Robert W. & Hoover, Roy W. et al., *The Five Gospels*. New York: Macmillan Publishing Company, 1993.

51. Dodd, Charles D., *The Parables of the Kingdom*. New York: Charles Scribner's Sons, 1961, p. 17.

"What's this I hear about you? Let's have an audit of your management, because your job is terminated."

which report the master's awareness of a long process of embezzlement.[52] Observing this dissension among Olympian exegetes, a mere mortal may understandably be emboldened (or impelled by hubris) to join in the fray.

But before we delve into the text, one more introductory observation is in order. The context of this passage is curious, but possibly revealing. The parable is found only in Luke, where it immediately follows "The Prodigal Son," which according to Luke 15:2–3 Jesus addressed to the Pharisees. Then in 16:1a, he turns and addresses the story of the shrewd manager to the disciples. And yet we are told in 16:14 that the Pharisees heard his remark about the love of money (verse 13) and sneered at him. Does the author wish us to imagine that on this occasion Jesus spoke to his followers in a loud enough stage whisper that he would be sure to be overheard? Such a possibility is not all that far-fetched, given the apparently continuous series of events from 14:1 through 16:15, a narrative that begins with Jesus going to dine with a leading Pharisee and immediately launching into a protracted attack (a somewhat unmannerly one, it appears from 14:1–14) on Pharisaic beliefs and practices. We shall return to this line of argument later.

Hear, Then, the Rest of the Parable

To define the steward's dilemma, narrate its resolution, and append a teaching to the story required but six verses:

> [3]Then the manager said to himself, "What am I going to do? My master is firing me. I'm not able to dig ditches and I'm ashamed to beg. [4]I've got it! I know what I'll do so doors will open for me when I'm removed from management."
> [5]So he called in each of his master's debtors. He said to the first, "How much do you owe my master?" [6]He said, "Five hundred gallons of olive oil."
> And he said to him, "Here is your invoice; sit down right now and make it two hundred and fifty." [7]Then he said to another, "And how much do you owe?"
> He said, "A thousand bushels of wheat." He says to him, "Here is your invoice; make it eight hundred." [8]The master praised the dishonest manager because he had acted prudently; for the children

---

52. Crossan, John Dominic, *In Parables*. Sonoma: Polebridge Press, 1992, p. 107.

of this world are more prudent in dealing with their own kind than are the children of light.

Whether Jesus' story ended with 16:7, 16:8a, or 16:8b, it is a simple enough chain of events. A wealthy man owns a large estate that is run by a boss farmer, who is either a servant or a slave. (His precise status will in the end prove less than crucial, but the reported termination of employment and the steward's need to arrange for his own future surely suggest a servant more than a slave.)[53] The manager's job is to oversee the entire agribusiness operation. He must determine the total yield of the grain, oil, wine, and livestock and assess the master's share; this he will collect and store, from it provide for the master's needs, then sell the surplus and turn over the profit.

This makes him a key figure in the institutionalized exploitation of the poor by the rich that with minor local variations characterized the pre-industrial world's socio-economic structure. Human nature being what it is, for such an agent to skim off a bit of the profit—if he could get away with it—was no doubt common practice. Call it incentive pay, or a primitive form of profit sharing. In a system where power authorizes appropriation, dishonesty may well be a matter of degree and perception. It is worth noting that the parable's several titles and the different translations variously describe the protagonist as astute, prudent, crafty, cunning, shrewd, unjust, and dishonest. Even more to the point, labels carrying positive and negative judgments are placed in matter-of-fact juxtaposition: although dishonest, the servant is commended for acting cleverly. One could almost imagine that the cleverness partly atoned for the misappropriation of funds. Indeed, one does encounter in literature both ancient and modern such nicely ambiguous locutions as "a cunning rogue" or "a charming villain." A fish must swim in its native pond; and one must render unto Caesar, the arch-symbol of systemic theft, what is his.

A Tale of Two Cultures

The manager who skims a little extra "commission" is like the poor: always with us. The practice is clearly attested in Chaucer's *Canterbury Tales*. One of the pilgrims is a reeve, the old English term for steward; and the game he played in the late 1300s was the same as it had been in Jesus' day.

---

53. Much the same argument appears in Via, Dan Otto Jr., *The Parables*. Philadelphia: Fortress Press, 1967, p. 157.

He knew the peasants' tricks and secrets well,
And so they feared him like the fires of hell.
Of his lord's rent he collected every nickel;
No auditor could catch him in a pickle.
But a nice share went to his secret coffer
Whence, if the need arose, he'd freely offer
The lord a loan of his own money, grain, or meat,
And get the profit, and a tip, and thanks—how neat![54]

How neat indeed, especially since after successfully working the system for many years he had attained the equivalent of middle-class status.

Another in the company was a manciple, an in-house caterer for a residential facility serving a group of London lawyers. High-powered and clever men they were; any one of them, Chaucer tells us, could manage the affairs of an entire shire at a good profit. But their clever steward made a nice profit for himself by purchasing supplies at discount prices—and, of course, billing at full market value. Hear Chaucer's comment:

Now isn't it a sure sign of God's grace
That one uneducated fellow could outpace
The wisdom of some thirty learned men,
And beat them at their game in their own den![55]

To be sure, Chaucer's approval is often ironic (even the thoroughly despicable Pardoner was "a good fellow"); but taken together, these two examples suggest that those who beat the rich and powerful at their own game received at least grudging admiration. Might it not have been so in Jesus' day?

Apparently, the steward in Jesus' tale got a little greedy or careless or unlucky, and someone informed on him. This is a more likely explanation than the lack of industry or efficiency to which some commentators assign his downfall. (Note that Chaucer's reeve always rode last in the procession; he knew enough people's secrets that he was in the habit of trusting no one.) At any rate, our steward was caught "exceeding the greed limit" and has been given the sack. Before the days of unemployment compensation, social security, and food stamps, losing one's job could be a dire circumstance—especially for a middle-level manager no longer strong enough for hard labor, and reluctant to be reduced to the

---

54. My rendering; it is hardly literal, but true to the content and spirit of the original.
55. Idem.

shame of beggary. What's to be done? He quickly hatches a contingency plan: he will allow the tenant farmers to discount their promissory notes, with the understanding that they'll return the favor by looking after him in his time of need. True, he had been doing well partly at their expense, but he was, after all, a fellow victim of the system and a fellow member of the permanent underclass; they'd see that he didn't starve.

So far, the story is eminently believable; no doubt it portrayed a common enough happenstance. As Mahlon Smith has observed, the events in Jesus' parables "had to be . . . recognizable . . . on the social horizons of both author and audience."[56] It would not be surprising to learn that Jesus knew of just such a case.

A Surprising Development?

What at first does seem surprising is that the master shrugged off the theft and commended the chicanery. After all, it was his money the manager had been pocketing, and his produce the scoundrel traded for future security. Hence the dilemma that has so long discomfited the pious: one may choose how to punctuate the passage and whether to capitalize the ambiguous *kyrios* (master or lord),[57] but neither option produces a morally uplifting conclusion.

One reading would have Luke saying that Jesus approved of the double theft: "The Master [Jesus] praised the dishonest manager because he had acted prudently . . ." The other reading would have Jesus himself saying that it's permissible to compound theft with fraud if you're in a sufficiently desperate fix: "The master praised the dishonest manager because he had acted prudently . . ."

Perhaps those will be less scandalized who recall the ample gospel attestation to Jesus' keen sympathy with the plight of the Palestinian peasantry. And Crossan provides a compelling insight into such a situation when he quotes an Irish tenant farmer dispossessed in 1836: "The poor would rather lose their lives, when driven to such desperation, than quietly submit to be ejected . . . for they have no other means of living. . . ."[58]

---

56. Smith, Mahlon H., "Israel's Prodigal Son: Reflections on Reimagining Jesus." Westar Institute Seminar Papers, Fall 1997, p. 76.

57. Ancient Greek did not have quotation marks and did not distinguish lower-case and uppercase letters, a fact which forces modern translators to make those decisions.

58. Crossan, *The Birth of Christianity*. San Francisco: Harper San Francisco, 1998, p. 169.

Then there arises the problem of verse 8b:

> . . . for the children of this world are more prudent in dealing with their own kind than are the children of light.

Was it Jesus or Luke who went on to explain the owner's approval by observing that people who have to sweat and hustle for a living appreciate the harsh facts of life better than those who follow a spiritual path? (Or who adopt a religious lifestyle to make it look that way. Is someone directing a stage whisper at Pharisees here?) Maybe those who fully understand the way the game is played recognize that one kind of theft often begets, even though it may not entirely justify, another.

Clearly, the crux of the interpretive problem is whether to see verses 8a and 8b as the words of Jesus or of Luke. To that question we now turn, considering the two parts of the verse in reverse order.

Maybe Not So Surprising

I defer to the experts that in 16:8b we have Luke speaking, but I would not be surprised if it had been Jesus. For one thing, it is a valid observation. Having worked for a number of years as an auto mechanic and a stone mason, I daresay I can get on with people in those trades better than, say, the average lawyer or theologian. Common experience gives us a common language and a bond of understanding. We accept one another as people who have lived the same life and dealt with the same problems. I'll bet that the peasant Jesus had more compassion for farmers—even boss farmers—than most Pharisees did. Or than most scholastics do.

That leads to a related point. One danger of focusing overmuch on the transcendent Christ is that we all too easily lose sight of the earthly (and sometimes earthy) Jesus who trod the dusty roads of Palestine to deliver a message that had to be put into words and images that common people could understand and relate to. That means he had to be a realist, a pragmatist, at times one of the "children of this world" in order to win people's acceptance and trust; for unless he could meet them in their world, he could not hope to enable them to catch a glimpse of that other order of being. The synoptic gospels abound in common-sense, axiomatic teachings: (my parapharases)

> The sun and the rain benefit the good and the evil alike. (Matt 5:45)
> Figs don't grow on thorn bushes, nor grapes on brambles. (Matt 7:16)
> If you aren't sick, you don't need a doctor. (Matt 9:12)

> Don't be fooled by show-offs. (Mark 12:38–40)
>
> If wealth is your number one concern, God must be number two—or lower. (Matt 6:24)
>
> A hundred dollars is less to a rich man than a buck to a beggar. (Mark 12:43–44)

An admittedly quick canvass of the red and pink passages in *The Five Gospels*—that is, the sayings judged most likely to be authentic—indicates that sayings of this sort outnumber the specifically ethical and religious directives by about two to one. And to them I would add what I take to be one of the lessons imbedded in "The Crafty Steward":

> To survive in this world, you sometimes have to play by the world's rules—and they aren't always fair.

Bornkamm puts a similar spin on the parable when he says, "Wisdom consists not in being indignant, but in being prepared."[59] A like sentiment informs Robert Frost's somewhat Machiavellian counsel:

> Better to go down dignified
> With boughten friendship at your side
> Than none at all. Provide, provide![60]

Jesus would have understood that; it is evident that he was all too aware of the personally and spiritually stultifying indignities his people suffered.

Maybe No Surprise at All

Considerably more important than the source of verse 8b, however, is that of 8a:

> The master praised the dishonest manager because he had acted prudently . . .

But in a way the case is much the same. Whether it is Jesus or Luke speaking is of more interest to scholars than to preachers. For whether Jesus uttered it or not, he might have. Indeed, he might as well have. The only good reason I can see for assigning verse 8a to Luke is to buttress an argument that Jesus' style was characteristically aphoristic as well as paradoxical. For verse 8a is essentially redundant. Ostensibly it tells us that the landowner approved of his steward's most recent shenanigans, but that skirts the real question: What was Jesus' opinion; what was

---

59. Bornkamm, p. 88.

60. Frost, Robert, "Provide, Provide." *Complete Poems*. New York: Henry Holt and Company, 1995, p. 404.

his point? After all, it's his parable. The obvious fact is that The Master agreed with the master. Given that the storyteller had some while since hung out his shingle as a moral sage and religious teacher, the very lack of any condemnation of the steward or dire punishment narratively visited upon him is pretty solid indication of approval. Absent an indictment, all charges must be considered dropped. Thus, even if all of verse 8 could be proven to be a Lukan gloss, it would still be in perfect harmony with Jesus' parable. Whoever made the statement, it is simply an explicit conclusion to what is implicit in the story.

An Objection

"Hold on a minute," I can hear you saying at this point, "even if one can temporarily suspend disbelief and for a moment see Jesus as a champion of the poor who could excuse this embezzlement (I know he was into forgiveness in a big way), I simply can't imagine the landowner putting up with it, never mind commending the embezzler for using his wits to commit a second theft." And it must be admitted that if the narrative flunks the reality test, it is neither a parable nor an effective medium of instruction. Many have found it simply incredible that the master—or The Master—should approve. (Though if the master could, who will argue that The Master should not?) I submit that they may have overlooked a fact so simple that it seems to have remained hidden by its obviousness.

Time is of the Essence

None of the commentaries I have read made any mention of the time factor. Consider the steward's problem. As soon as he is fired, he concocts a strategy for survival. But it requires him to contact a number of farmers who owe his master a share of their produce and get them to rewrite their IOUs. Being a nitpicker by nature and training, I wonder how many Jewish Mediterranean peasants could write. But be that as it may, however the deed was done, it would surely not be the work of a few minutes to locate a farmer, have him travel from his field to the owner's farmstead, explain the situation, convince a naturally suspicious rustic that he wouldn't be getting himself into as much trouble as the steward was in, then get some sort of commitment about the expected *quid pro quo*, and finally fix or forge the necessary records. How many indebted tenants were there? How many could he deal with in a day? How long did it take for the master to learn what he was up to?

If we assume a reasonable number of debtors and assign a reasonable amount of time to each of the necessary steps, it is difficult to imagine arrangements being completed in less than a week. (Would not the apparently delayed audit reflect the master's recognition—or insistence—that individual farmers must check and confirm their reported debt? Would he not otherwise become suspicious of the unusual comings and goings and consultations?) All of this suggests that in the days that elapsed between his angry firing of the steward and his perhaps grudging commendation of the man's resourcefulness, the master had plenty of time to ruminate on the past and wonder about the future. And granted the considerable difference in their social standing, it is hard to imagine that the master would give no thought to the fate of his old and once trustworthy servant—one whose worst crime, after all, may have been overstepping the accepted boundaries in the all but universal human pursuit of material security. Besides, they go back a long way together, and their worlds do overlap considerably. They have worried together about sun and rain and crop prices; they have both cursed locusts, excessive taxation, and the ravages of armed conflict. And the master would be a hard man indeed if it never occurred to him that he would hate to dig or beg.

In an op-ed article a few years ago, Harvey Wichman, a psychology professor at Claremont McKenna College, noted the likely relation of time and empathy:

> Probably the single most important study on forgiveness to date recently reported that empathy for the perpetrator is a necessity for forgiveness to take place. No empathy, no forgiveness. What is more, any empathy is empathy.
> It doesn't have to be related to the offense. . . . Research also shows that anger that interferes with forgiving slowly disappears with time . . . [and] is matched with a steady increase in the likelihood of forgiveness.[61]

So the master fires his steward because business is business and rules are rules and honor is honor. But people are people, and the best rule sometimes has to be applied with mercy. The absence of any mention of further punishment or even contemplation of it surely implies compassion. The commendation in verse 8a is an explicit suggestion of forgiveness. It could spring in part from a feeling of relief that the old fellow would be looked after. That would be compassion.

---

61. Wichman, Harvey, "What does it take to forgive?" *The Providence Journal*, October 18, 1998.

To be sure, one has a somewhat uneasy feeling about subjecting a piece of oral literature to the intense scrutiny that might be appropriate for a carefully crafted poem. A possible defense is that others have done as much. For example, Brandon Scott and Dan Via contribute a great deal to our understanding of the possible resonances of this parable by seeing it derived from a picaresque repertoire, or as an example of the trickster-dupe subtype of that genre.[62] Still, it is just possible that here we have an account of an actual event. (Fifty to a hundred years ago, no doubt, actual encounters took place between traveling salesmen and farmers' daughters. Some may have had surprise endings—like a salesman turning farmer.) And if the steward's tale reflects a real occurrence, its surprise ending may have been what recommended it as an addition to Jesus' repertoire. Or he might have added that twist to challenge his hearers to reconsider their assumptions. As Julian Hills incisively argues with reference to this parable, "God's domain . . . is a time when loyalties are divided, old allegiances called into question—who's right? who's wrong?"[63] A more oblique defense is this: I recall Robert Frost insisting on the open-endedness of a poem; like that of a true parable, its meaning is in some measure what you make of it.[64]

The words "compassion" and "forgiveness" do not appear in the text of the parable, but even if we consider only verses 1–7, the qualities these words represent are central to the dramatic action. Perhaps one of the crucial points the story makes is that the children of this world are sometimes most able to forgive because they have themselves felt or seen the importance of forgiveness. They know that one has to be "creative" to survive under a confiscatory system, and hence they accord to the survivor a degree of empathy, and even admiration.

Beware the Leaven of the Pharisees

Inability to forgive means that you have put yourself on a higher plane than others, that you in effect claim to be living by a different set of rules, under a different dispensation. Your God doesn't recognize those other people, so you don't have to either. You've worked hard to become nearly perfect; they should, too. It is worth noting, I think, that such a description nicely fits the Pharisee at the temple, who thanks God that

---

62. Scott, Bernard Brandon, *Hear then the Parable*. Minneapolis: Fortress Press, 1989, pp. 259–265; and Via, pp. 159–161.
63. Hills, Julian V., "Jesus: Towards a Silhouette." *Westar Institute Seminar Papers*, Fall 1996, pp. 45–46.
64. Frost, Reading and lecture at Dartmouth College, 1954.

he is superior to that grubby publican (Luke 18:11–12). Remembering Jesus' estimate of him, one recalls the Pharisees who sneered at Jesus in 16:14 and his condemnation of their self-importance in 16:15:

> [14]The Pharisees, who were money-grubbers, heard all this and sneered at him. [15]But he said to them, "you're the type who justify yourselves to others, but God reads your hearts: what people rank highest is detestable in God's estimation."

Perhaps we find this parable so difficult because it is radically subversive of the wisdom of this world: it condones a material sin to exalt a spiritual virtue, and paradoxically invokes this world's wisdom to do so. That makes all Pharisees uneasy.

It has been correctly observed that just as the parable of the Wheat and the Darnel (Matt 13:24–30) is not about farming methods, so the Crafty Steward is not about agribusiness administration[65]—or, one might add, about golden parachutes. In fact, the usual titles may have focused our attention on the wrong person. The central event in the action is one that is not reported, but implied: the change of heart shown by the magnanimous master. Thus I submit that the parable may be a disturbing but powerful lesson on the necessity of forgiveness, a spiritual exercise arising from the love of neighbor. And that, we have on good authority, is like unto the love of God.

---

65. Crossan, *In Parables*, p. 63.

Rants and Raves

Having assailed biblical authors for altering the work of their predecessors to suit their own views, I may be on shaky ground in suggesting that a few portions of both the Hebrew and Christian scriptures should consigned to the chopping block. But if one combines Luther's eminently defensible proposal that Revelation be stricken from the Bible with his wrong-headed description of the letter of James as "an epistle of straw" worthy of the same fate, one might be granted a bit of wiggle-room in such matters.

I have already alluded to my distaste for Luke's "quoting" Paul to the effect that God was in the process of transferring his divine aegis from Judaism to Gentile Christianity. What had Jews done to deserve this? Some had not been persuaded by Paul's preaching to accept Jesus as the Son of God. Luke was no doubt unaware of the result that such a proclamation might have on Justin Martyr or Augustine of Hippo or Luther, or the extremes to which it would be taken in the twentieth century, but shouldn't honest Christians openly repudiate the idea? Couldn't every new Bible at least include a footnote explaining Luke's blasphemous supersessionism and rejecting its doctrinal standing?

A similar handling might be applied to Matthew's story in which a Jewish crowd calls for Jesus' death and absolves Pilate of any guilt: "His blood be on us and our children!" (Matt 27:25). The entire narrative (Matt 27:11–26) is as patently fictitious as it is slanderous, and that's the problem. A fiction can be harmless—as the report that Jesus was born to a virgin in Bethlehem—if it does not promote or incite harmful actions; or it can be morally reprehensible (like Matthew's calumny) if it does. Of course a fiction can also be morally uplifting, as in the case of Jesus' parables. But it seems to me that to protect the Bible's reputation as a sacred text, every homilist should feel obliged early in every ministry to point out the perfidy of this Matthean invention.

And I have a problem with Revelation 19:11–21 because of its depiction of Christ ("the Word of God", "King of kings, Lord of lords") wearing a bloody robe, wielding a sharp sword with which to "strike down the nations," and casting the armies of evil into "a lake of fire that burns with sulfur." This is a grotesquely distorted depiction of the Prince of Peace whose great commandment was love of God and neighbor. It seems ironically appropriate that in 22:7, 12, and 20 the author reiterates God's assurance that all this will happen soon; for since it hasn't occurred in two millennia, I propose that we now accept the book's self-cancellation notice and so inform any who might take its prophecies as anything more than a sacrilegious aberration.

Two more blots on the Christian escutcheon should be noted. The first is the systematic assignment of women to subordinate status. Half of Jesus' followers have suffered from male domination; and strange as it may seem, the one commonly made responsible for this is Paul, who famously declared equality of the two sexes (Gal 3:28) and described a number of women as leaders as leaders in his churches (Phil 4:2–3; Rom 16:1, 3, 6, 12). The primary textual foundation for his subordination of women is 1 Cor 14:34–35:

> . . . women should be silent in all the churches. For they are not permitted to speak, but should be subordinate, as the law also says. If there is anything they desire to know, let them ask their husbands at home. For it is shameful for a woman to speak in church.

A further denigration of women appears in 1 Cor 11:3–16, and the forged deuterocanonicals (Ephesians, Colossians, 1&2 Timothy and Titus) have parallel examples aplenty. So what's going on here?

The eminent Paul scholar, William O. Walker Jr. makes a compelling case that the two 1 Corinthians passages are later interpolations by Pauline "followers" who, like the deuterocanonical authors, rejected Paul's radical equality.[66] Perhaps it's about time that these crippling distortions of Christian doctrine were laid to rest. Shouldn't they at least be flagged and explained in footnotes? If not, Paul's apparent self-contradiction and his falsely assigned responsibility for a crime against humanity are unlikely to get past the pulpit and into the pews.

For me, at least, an even more difficult problem arises from Romans 10:9:

> . . . because if confess with your lips that Jesus is Lord and believe in your heart that God raised him from the dead, you will be saved.

Not only does this (like Rom 3:28) appear to contradict Romans 2:6–8,

> For [God] will repay according to each one's deeds: to those who by patiently doing good seek for glory and honor and immortality, he will give eternal life; while for those who are self-seeking and who obey not truth but wickedness, there will be wrath and fury.

---

66. Walker, William O. Jr, *Some Surprises form the Apostle Paul*, pp. 59, 65–67, 97–100.

but it also denies the correctness of Jesus' clear preference for deeds over words:

> Why do you call me 'Lord, Lord, and not do what I say? (Luke 6:46; and see vv. 47–49)

Romans 10:9 fails the acid test of doctrinal validity because it promises salvation (whatever one may take that to involve) on the basis of belief and the verbal expression thereof. Granted, the problem results in part from a dubious translation: the pivotal word "believe" is a rendering of the Greek verb *pisteuo*, which can imply conditions ranging from opinion to belief to unconditional trust. In a religious context it might well suggest something more like the latter than the former, but Christianity seems always to have preferred "faith" and "belief" to "trust"—or even better, I think, "commitment." It is interesting to note that Martin Luther chose to render the related noun *pistis* as *Glaube* (belief) rather than *Vertrauen*, ("trust", "confidence") when translating the author he most admired.

But like his hero, Luther was a niche marketer, and knew the honey of Heaven would prove more attractive than the vinegar of discipleship. The catch, of course, was that while issuing tickets at a discount rate proved good for membership rolls, it required a considerable dilution of Jesus' message. Perhaps it was a necessary compromise. Still, as we today face a greater challenge than Paul could have dreamed of, a similar question looms: Do we seek an easy answer to our existential conundrum or accept the challenge of discipleship? I suspect that Paul Gilk is right when he says that if Christianity—or indeed humankind—is to survive, both must adopt a simple but demanding mantra: "servanthood and stewardship."[67] We cannot expect much help from a product of our imagination.

Nor is the Hebrew Bible free of troublesome passages. Knowing that much of its pre-exilic portions reflect a Late Bronze or Early Iron Age culture, I am less inclined to chafe at minor outrages, but several grave problems need to be addressed. And even making allowances for Judaism's polytheistic and henotheistic roots, it is unsettling to read of a God whose first experiment with humanity was such a failure that he decided to cancel the experiment—but then at the last minute persuaded himself to try again with a new cast of actors. Genesis 6:11–8:19 tells the story in two different versions.

---

67. Gilk, Paul, *Picking Fights with the Gods*, pp. 129, 232.

And this depiction of a somewhat inept deity is before long followed by that of a Jahweh/Elohim who slaughters every firstborn in the land of Egypt in order to compel Pharaoh to set his chosen people free (Exod 11:4–5). Then a few decades later he employs a program of genocide to enable them to resettle a land they had left some five centuries earlier:

> When the Lord your God brings you into the land you are about to enter and occupy, . . . then you must utterly destroy them. Make no covenant with them and show them no mercy." (Deut 7:1–2) So Joshua defeated the whole land . . . he left no one remaining but utterly destroyed all that breathed, as the Lord God of Israel had commanded. (Josh 10:40)

One cannot help but wonder how many people have left the church because these grotesque blasphemies were not explained and laid to rest.

Last of all, one is hard put to explain the final two verses of Psalm 137. After a tender paean memorializing the time of Exile, the psalmist calls on the Lord to recall he enmity of the Edomites who cheered on the Babylonian conquerors in 587 BCE (at least 50 years earlier) and ends with a bitter curse:

> O daughter Babylon . . . Happy shall they be who pay you back what you have done to us! . . . who take your little ones and dash them against the rock!

What sort of God inspired this grisly malediction? Doesn't someone owe his modern worshippers an explanation of this blasphemous passage?

But there is much to inspire hope. Surely Christianity need not find it dangerous to recognize that most of the authors of the anthology we call the Bible were visionaries, idealists, enthusiasts—promoters and defenders of abstract belief systems. Is it so surprising that the Renaissance, the Enlightenment, and the resulting modern worldview have left any notions of the inerrancy of Scripture in tatters? Yet much of inestimable value remains, and simple honesty requires our turning from rants to raves. A few hurrahs must be sounded.

Let the first be for Micah 6:8:

> . . . what does the Lord require of you but to do justice,
> to love kindness, and to walk humbly with your God?

This little gem, often called the Old Testament's Golden Rule, sums up in unambiguous terms what the religious life—that is, the good life—calls upon us to do. It offers clear and simple marching orders; no creeds, no doctrines, no pious protestations. One might well recall the Zoroastrian commandment, "Good thoughts, good words, good actions." That's what it's all about, folks.

And of great value is the presence of two radically contradictory creation stories: the ancient myth of Genesis 2:4b—3:22 and the almost modern hypothetical proposal of Genesis 1:1–2:4a that dates to the Exile period at least a millennium later. Those, together with the conflicting details of the two interwoven Flood stories (Gen 6:5–8:22), warn us against the dangers of reading scriptural narratives as historical accounts. And the three irreconcilable references to the legendary Goliath (1Sam 17; 2 Sam 21:19; and 1 Chron 20:5–7) should serve to clinch the point. It is no small thing to be relieved of an obligation to find literal facts where none were intended or even possible.

Those who recognize that the sacred and the secular are elements of a continuum must also be ready to tip our hats to the prophetic books, for their authors were often as much involved in politics as in religion. Isaiah 1:10–20, which makes ethical demands of those who wish for political and social gratification, is a fine example. Another is the poorly translated and misrepresented advice by which the same prophet assures King Ahaz that he need not fear a threatening northern alliance: "Look, the young woman is with child, and shall bear a son . . . [and] before the child knows how to refuse the evil and choose the good, the land before whose two kings you are in dread will be deserted." The issue is political and immediate, not theological and seven centuries in the future. And even more surprising is a statement in Second Isaiah: "Thus says the Lord to his anointed, to Cyrus, whose right hand I have grasped to subdue nations . . ." (Is 45:1). A Persian Messiah, no less: quite a blending of politics and theology!

Nor should we forget Habakkuk, who inveighs against the systemic greed and pride that lead the wealthy to so oppress their neighbors as to incite violent retribution (2:4–12). Or Amos, who sarcastically invites Israel's enemies to observe the internal turmoil that will render her easy prey (3:9–11).

Here we turn from prophets to Proverbs, a long and often tedious catalogue of commonsense counsel and everyday ethics sprinkled with assurances that the Lord guarantees their validity. This may not sound like "rave" material, but in addition to enjoying a number of memorable aphorisms, the non-theist reader may be pleased to recognize a concept that resembles Lao Tzu's vision of the unseen creative and regulative dynamic of all things—the Tao.

Take my instruction instead of silver, and knowledge rather than choice gold;
for wisdom is better than jewels . . . (8:10–11a)

One who spares words is knowledgeable; one who is cool in spirit has understanding. (17:27)

Those with good sense are slow to anger, and it is their glory to overlook an offense. (19:11)

Even children make themselves known by their acts,
by whether what they do is pure and right. (20:11)

Whoever digs a pit will fall into it, and a stone will come back on the one who starts it rolling. (26:27)

And finally we should cheer for an ancient text that corrects the oft-repeated canard of Jesus' unique exhortation to love one's enemy:

If your enemies are hungry, give them bread to eat;
if they are thirsty, give them water to drink; (25:21)

Alas, his prophet-predecessor appends a mean-spirited motive to such acts of charity:

For you will heap coals of fire on their heads, and the Lord will reward you. (25:22)

One might wonder just which act the Lord will be rewarding, but the command to treat enemies with respect and humanity is a bright spot in a dark world. And here, as in the case of the vengeful psalmist who wished death upon innocent Babylonian babies, we are apparently dealing with ethical sensibilities that had not fully evolved. Still, the horrific misery of today's third-world populations forbids us to claim true moral maturity.

Two more cheers for Jewish texts are in order. The first is Susannah and the Judgment of Daniel (Dan 13[JB]). Its only relation to the canonical book is the legendary title character, who though here only a boy is inspired both to challenge two elders who have insidiously condemned to death a young woman who refused their sexual advances and to devise a clever plan by which to expose their wickedness. Often hailed as the world's first detective story, it sometimes appears as the first chapter in the book because of his youth. He also plays the sleuth in Bel and the Dragon (Dan 14 [JB]), a less interesting but amusing fantasy in which priestly corruption is unmasked and an altered version of the lion pit incident (Dan 6) is added. Be that as it may, the story of Susannah does little to support the Bible's traditional description as "holy" or "sacred"; it simply sparkles as a narrative gem depicting the triumph of good over evil.

The second is a problematic text earlier mentioned in passing, but one of supreme importance for any discussion of the Judeo-Christian scriptures. Lloyd Geering, an Old Testament scholar and former head of New Zealand's Presbyterian Seminary, informs us that Christians did not suppress Ecclesiastes because it was part of the Hebrew Bible, and Jewish acceptance reflected ". . . not the validity of its religious ideas, but the belief that it had been written by Solomon."[68]

But why would anyone seek to ban Ecclesiastes? Because, he observes, despite its "churchy" title, this book ". . . completely undermines much of what is traditionally preached from Christian pulpits. Its message is quite impossible to reconcile with most of the rest of the Bible. Indeed, it openly questions the validity of the doctrine . . . that God rules this universe in a loving way that ensures justice for all. More than any other book in the canon, Ecclesiastes provides clear evidence that the Bible is a collection of books that are not only of human origin but reflect human thought and experience."[69] What greater boon could an unbiased student of religion ask than the witness of an ancient seeker of truth who challenges the ancient assumptions of supernaturalism and divine inspiration?

Now let us turn to several Christian texts that some may find equally disturbing, but which elicit from me a few hearty kudos for New Testament authors. One of my favorites passages is Luke 17: 20–21, in which Jesus says that the coming of God's kingdom will not be a visible event; rather, the term names a condition the potential for which resides within and all around us. It will arrive when or to the degree that we perfect our lives: he can point the Way, but we must walk it. Jesus was a realist: his God does not issue free passes.

And he was human to the core. That's why I like John 1:14a— ". . . the Word became flesh and pitched his tent among us." Yes, that's what the Greek text actually says, and why for me it has a deeper meaning than the author intended.

On the same theme, I would argue, is the famous story of Jesus and the Syro-Phoenecian woman who asked him to cure her sick daughter

---

68. Geering, Lloyd, *Such is Life,* p. 10.
69. Ibid.

(Mk 7:24–30). When he refused on the grounds that his mission was to feed "the children" (i.e., of Israel), she pulled him up short by observing that even the little dogs under the table get a few crumbs thrown to them. He granted the validity of her witty retort by curing the girl then and there. To be sure, the story is almost certainly fictitious, but I am heartened to imagine that Jesus could so graciously acknowledge his gaffe and respond appropriately to a reasonable reprimand.

Passages in both Mark and Luke go so far as to suggest that his contemporaries at times worried about his sanity or took offense at his teaching. Obviously, these could have been omitted, and could well be fictitious, but they do depict him as a fallible human being, and as such someone in whom we can believe. In Mark 3:2 his family worry that he has lost his mind, and they try to control him; in Luke 4:28–30 members of a synagogue congregation are so outraged by his suggestion that God might care as much for Gentiles as for Jews that they try to throw him over a cliff! Here of course we have a Lukan theme (cf. Acts 28:23–28) and a fiction, but in both cases one is compelled to see him as a man rather than a divine being.

In each of the three synoptic gospels we find the chreia about a man who ran up to Jesus and asked what he must do to inherit eternal life (Mark 10:17–22, Matt19:16–22, Luke 18:18–23). The three performances vary little, though the original text by Mark has always annoyed me. (In it, the man assures Jesus that he has kept all the commandments since he was a child, and we are told that thereupon Jesus looked at him and loved him. Sorry, but I cannot believe that Jesus was such a sucker for a ridiculous claim.) And the lesson is always the same: Keeping the commandments is not enough; one must share one's wealth with the poor and needy.

Unfortunately, few are familiar with a fourth text of the story, for it appeared in an early work that was lost or suppressed. Fortunately, what is now known as Gospel of the Nazoreans 6 was recorded by the third-century church father Origen:

1. The second rich man said to him, "Teacher, what good do I have to do to live?"
2. He said to him, "Mister, follow the Law and the Prophets." He answered, "I've done that." He said to him, "Go sell everything you own and give it away to the poor and then come follow me."
3. But the rich man didn't want to hear this, and began to scratch his head. And the Lord said to him, "How can you say that you

follow the Law and the Prophets? In the Law it says, 'Love your neighbor as yourself.'

4. Look around you: many of your brothers and sisters, sons and daughters of Abraham, are living in filth and dying of hunger. Your house is full of good things and not a thing of yours manages to get out to them."

5. Turning to his disciple Simon who was sitting with him, he said, "Simon, son of Jonah, it's easier for a camel to squeeze through a needle's eye than for a wealthy person to get into heaven's domain."

Clearly, this is the version we should frame and pass on: the introduction is noteworthy for its brevity; the reluctance of the man totally understandable; the verisimilitude of his gesture both amusing and dramatic; Jesus' detailed and biting reprimand has the ring of authenticity; and the final statement employs striking Semitic exaggeration to drive the point home. What an exquisite example of the genre!

Thomas 42, the shortest saying attributed to Jesus, is almost as cryptic as it is brief: "Be passersby", "Become itinerants", or "Become wanderers"—pick your translation. It is often seen as belonging to a theme of radical itinerancy—cf. ". . . give the money to the poor and come, follow me" (Mark 10:21) and "Go on your way [but] carry no purse, bag, or sandals" (Luke 10:3–4). Or consider Stephen Patterson's reading of the imperative: "If you are in the imperial web of brokerage and patronage, get out of it."[70] Today some might see an exhortation to reject a capitalist web of financial power and political influence: if you're part of the rat race, drop out, practice servanthood and stewardship. Such advice lacks popular appeal, but empire proved to be a flawed system and humanity's present course is clearly unsustainable. Or the saying could seem a call to holiness, an assertion that "to have life and have it more abundantly" we must minimize our quotidian concerns and prioritize those pursuits that help us to transcend mediocrity. After all, what has taken a hundred thousand years of cultural evolution to create should not be carelessly discarded. In any case, Thomas 42 is a valuable reminder that we harbor a higher calling.

And while we're on the subject of Thomas, let's give a brief but rousing cheer to Jim Robinson and Charlie Hedrick for their indispensable roles in making this text widely available. For not only do about half

---

70. Patterson, Stephen J., *The God of Jesus,* p. 65.

the sayings of Jesus it reports have canonical parallels, but the Thomas reading often suggests an earlier version free from later Christian allegorizing. In fact, one might reasonably argue that a basic understanding of Thomas' place in the development of the tradition is essential for any who proclaim the Gospel.

Two other non-canonical Christian writings deserve favorable recognition. The first is *The Gospel of Mary of Magdala*, an early second-century text of interest because it portrays the title character as the disciple closest to Jesus, and the one commissioned to explain his teachings to the others. And after Jesus' departure her primacy is reinforced when, after Andrew and Peter question her truthfulness and authority, Levi rebukes Peter for his wrathfulness and failure to accept Jesus' high opinion of Mary. The rest then confirm her leadership by going forth to preach the Lord's message.[71] Also noteworthy is the work's Gnostic eschatology. It depicts humans as spiritual entities that have descended from the divine realm, have taken on human form, and upon the death of the body seek to return to their celestial home. But their way is beset by contrary spirits who, much like airport security guards, control their right to pass to the gate. Only those who demonstrate lives of spiritual and moral achievement by proper responses to one or more challenges get to "fly." This seems to me a better metaphor for the process of salvation than the traditional Christian idea, for I see the "guardians" as representing the people we daily encounter along our way, and the judgment of our worthiness as dependent on how we treat those we meet. "A nip and a sip" may be a useful or comforting performance, but rituals are only symbols. Our spiritual health is attested by the respect and concern we show for others.

A second non-biblical and similarly little-known example of important early Christian literature is *The Didache*, or *The Teaching of the Twelve [Disciples]*. Though surely a misnomer, the title bespeaks the serious attempt of an early Jewish-Christian community to define its dedication to what it considered the essence of Jesus' message. Portions of the text may point to a mid-first century composition, some elements to a setting in the early second. Half the text is a catalogue of ethical demands and prohibitions; several chapters define proper ritual performance and treatment of visitors and prospective members. Of particular interest are Chapters Nine and Ten, two parallel but clearly variant eucharistic texts. In the former we find verbally parallel thanks to David and Jesus for the gift of the vine and thanks to Jesus for bread:

---

71. King, Karen, *The Gospel of Mary of Magdala*, pp. 117–18.

9:2 First, concerning the cup:
We give you thanks, our Father,
for the holy vine of your servant David
which you revealed to us through your servant Jesus . . .

9:3 And concerning the broken loaf:
We give you thanks, our Father,
for the life and knowledge
which you revealed to us through your servant Jesus . . .

And only in the doxology that ends 9:4 do we find the honorific title "Christ":

Because yours is the glory and the power
through Jesus Christ forever.[72]

Though it does not repeat that term, Chapter Ten may reflect a later revision, since David's role is all but eliminated, and Jesus' has been upgraded; we now give thanks for "food and drink and eternal life through your servant Jesus" (10:3). Two things are clear: First, *The Didache* reflects a very low christology, apparently indicating that the community was not ready for a Son of God or a divine Savior. Rather than a guarantee of immortality, they took Jesus' example to offer a path to *zoon aionion*—the life of the age, a perfected life. Second, it reflects a very early form of eucharistic practice—giving thanks for food and drink with no hint of the Pauline embellishment in which the bread and wine become symbols of Jesus' martyrdom.

Ah, if only we might recall that *eucharistia* meant "a giving of thanks" and thus come to recapture the healthy simplicity of these early followers of the Way!

My penultimate nominee for a text that demands our gratitude is the Letter of James. It was long thought to be the work of James, the brother of Jesus who led the Jerusalem community early in the first century. The problem is that it demonstrates a sophisticated mastery of Greek style that would be all but impossible for a Galilean peasant to have achieved. But an educated follower could have recorded and rewritten an oral declamation; after all, we know that almost all of Paul's letters were dictated to a scribe. And strongly indicative of a Jamesian source is the content of the letter: it is a blunt repudiation of Paul's doctrine of salvation by faith alone, and thus a reflection of the Mother Church's view that Paul's dismissal of a number of basic Jewish teachings and practices amounted

---

72. Milavec, Aaron, *The Didache*, p. 23.

to dangerous heresy. But whoever may have written or edited this epistle, it cannot be denied that just as Ecclesiastes undermines much of the Hebrew Bible, James mounts a solid attack on the very foundation of the Pauline letters—thirteen of the twenty-seven books of the Christian canon. The key argument appears in James 2:17: "So faith by itself, if it has no works, is dead." That's pretty hard to deny. And since Jesus didn't tell his followers what doctrines they should believe but how they should behave, I'm ready to cheer with anyone who cheers for James.

Speaking of undermining the authority of the scriptures, Robert Miller, editor of Westar's bimonthly *The Fourth R*, recently brought to his readers' attention that Jesus was perhaps the greatest whistle-blower of all.[73] It was, he shows, a fundamental assumption of Judaism that God controlled the natural forces of sun and rain to reward his people for keeping their covenantal bargains, and to punish them when they strayed. And both the Jewish and Christian scriptures assured the faithful of God's 'carrot and stick' use of his power to enforce his will (see, e.g., Joel 2: 23–24, Zechariah14:17, and Acts 5: 1–11). But in Matthew 5:45, Jesus informs us that ". . . [God] makes his sun rise on the evil and on the good, and sends rain on the righteous and the unrighteous." As Miller observes, this radical aphorism questions the most fundamental of traditional biblical values in a disarmingly gentle way—by simply stating an obvious fact that many are unwilling to acknowledge. Maybe it's time we gave further thought to some of our unexamined religious postulates.

P.S:

1. Kudos to the editors of the New Revised Standard Version for noting that the Greek original translated "faith" might well (or better?) be rendered "faithfulness" and for a wealth of other explanatory footnotes.
2. Endless thanks to the editors of the Jerusalem Bible for their helpful introductory essays, detailed cross-references, and extensive footnoting.
3. Just as any serious reader of the Bible should become familiar with these texts, no diligent reader of the Gospels should be without *The Five* Gospels, Westar Institute's report of its eight-year study aimed at identifying the authentic sayings of Jesus.

---

73. Miller, Robert J., "Free Rain," *The Fourth R*, Jan-Feb2021.

Jottings

This unorthodox appendix represents an admittedly oblique contention that one can communicate the essence of Jesus' message without resorting to the several forms of outmoded discourse that I have challenged in the preceding treatise.

Occasional Ruminations
Holy Week

Yesterday was Palm Sunday, a time when the faithful are usually treated to a nugget or two of historical information and inundated with a great deal of evangelical treacle, but seldom if ever challenged to wonder about the protagonist's motives or intentions. The so-called 'triumphal entry' begins with Matthew's inept and unfortunately comical two-donkey adaptation (Matt 21:6–7) of a solemn one-donkey vision describing a *priestly* processional of some three centuries earlier (Zech 9:9)—for by then it had been that long since the last Israelite king was deposed in 587 BCE.

And Israel's long-frustrated dream of a Davidic king ruling in Jerusalem over a triumphant people not only led to a child of Galilean peasants being assigned a birthplace in Judea and hailed as a heaven-sent messiah, but enabled his proclamation as the savior of all mankind. As I have noted earlier, it required all the skill of myth-making evangelists to overcome the paradox of an anointed ruler crucified by the enemy he was expected to expel; but hope and repetition can work wonders.

The traditional liturgical texts and hymns of mainline churches illustrate the process. Jesus is hailed as king to whom glory, praise, and honor are due; but he was from one of the lowest social orders and was radically opposed to all forms of royalty and empire. He rejected praise (Luke 6:46) and urged his followers to serve others (Mark 10:43). The Jesus hailed as "redeemer king" and "David's royal son" is the product of the early church, as is the call to "crown him prophet, priest, and king." So also must be the appellation "God's only son," for his earliest followers were Jews, and would surely have considered that a blasphemy. Jesus seems to have preferred the modest "son of Adam"—which meant simply "human being." But scripture repeatedly reflects a time when kings needed to have praise lavished upon them and to be assured that their subjects wished them to live forever; expressions of that sort were *de rigueur* among those who wished to gain favor by professing loyalty. And although the habit persists to this day among those given to uncritical acceptance of traditional theology, I think Jesus would tell any so inclined to knock it off and instead take up deeds of justice, mercy, and charity.

Those who deem it sacrilegious to "blow the whistle" on the inconsistent accounts of Jesus' final week are invited to read *Inventing the Passion* by Arthur Dewey, a respected professor of theology and long-time Westar pal, who documents the cut-and-paste process by which passages from the Hebrew Bible were assembled to create the gospel stories—accounts written between forty and seventy years after the events by people who not only lacked personal knowledge but had little or no second-hand testimony to go on. But they had the Psalms; see 21:1; 22:18; 31:5; 69:21. As to what actually happened on that fateful Friday, Dom Crossan summed it up in one of his many incisive epigrams: "Those who knew didn't care, those who cared didn't know."

• • •

Kata Holon—It's all one universe

We spiritualize religion at our considerable peril, forgetting that Jesus' parable of the Leaven connotes the indivisibility of the sacred and the secular. I suspect that we do so in order to absolve ourselves of the moral responsibility to focus a good part of our lives on creating a better world. That is, we forget the lesson of Luke 17:21: that God's kingdom is all around us waiting to be realized. This further suggests that Paul Gilk is correct in calling for an added dimension of the Christian message. Jesus' central proclamation (*kerygma*) was the good news (*godspel*) of God's sovereign presence, the ultimate realization of which requires an active love of God and neighbor. But today that is not enough, for humankind has not only achieved the power to destroy the ecosystem and with it all life forms, but is well on the way to achieving that tragic and indeed satanic rejection of divine providence. Therefore, Gilk insists, along with answering Jesus' call to radical servanthood we must take up a burden he could not have imagined: the radical stewardship that is necessary to preserve the sacred gift of life.[74]

• • •

On personal impermanence

If I accept the fact that my life ends at death—that this earthly adventure is all I can expect—then any promises or threats concerning a future existence have no validity. And that means that any concept of salvation is restricted to discovering and realizing as much of the meaning and potential of my journey as I can. For while the effort may be

---

74. Gilk, Paul, *Picking Fights with the Gods*, p. 129.

inspired by the example of others, the result can never depend on what they may have done, but only on my response and commitment to the ideals they represent.

• • •

Tectonic Changes

In a recent article Dominic Kirkham notes two interesting parallels between the Reformation and Vatican II: both posed serious disruptions and challenges to devout believers, and both were attacked as attempts by a malicious minority to undermine a sacred tradition.

But the attacks were erroneous, says this learned former cleric, for ". . . in both the medieval and modern epochs, the whole epistemic and theological structure of the cultural world was disintegrating under the pressure of new knowledge and experience."[75]

• • •

"God" is not a being, but a symbol of the indwelling impulse toward self-transcendence that characterizes all things, and therefore a mythic entity. "Sin" and "sinfulness" are abstract nouns that serve to label certain human actions or proclivities as harmful or morally wrong; they are not ontological categories.

This is my impressionistic riff on a central theme of Lloyd Geering's article in *The (Presbyterian) Outlook* 25 September 1965—an article that was the first of four documents that led to the Assembly's proceedings against him in 1967.

(The entire fascinating record is available in the Sept-Oct 2015 issue of Westar's bi-monthly *The Fourth R.*)

• • •

As Crossan observes, Paul did not include Jesus in a biographical gospel, but encoded him in the myth of a savior who, as one Paul scholar notes, obviates the need for mortals to forgive or repent. As a result, profession of belief becomes the primary criterion, while behavior is of secondary importance.

In doing so, he derailed Christianity by founding it on creeds and doctrines, thus paving the way for a flood of speculative fictions by evangelists and clergy. Thus subverted, it rapidly attracted an ever-wider following.

• • •

"The basic plot of Buddhism is the story of enlightenment, a change of heart that changes everything else. In the official mythology this

---

75. *Sofia* #141, Sep. 2021.

transformation is a sudden clarification of view, an understanding that pours over you like summer rain."[76]

The "masterplot" of traditional Western Christianity is God's salvation of humankind, whose existential guilt was inherited from Adam and can be atoned for only by accepting the grace manifested in Jesus' sacrificial death and confirmed by his resurrection.

But Jesus preached the dawn of a new reality he called the Reign of God, the potential for which was already present though largely unrecognized, and the actualization of which required only *metanoia*: a new, more spiritual vision and a resulting change of heart that replaces selfishness with love.

What most people know as Christianity, then, would seem to represent a considerable distortion of the message of the crucified teacher from Nazareth, whose call to an enlightened life shows a greater resemblance to the doctrines of Gautama than to the religion created by others and misrepresented as his.

• • •

Notes for an Earth Day Sermon—April 19, 2020

Nature and nature's laws lay hid in night;
God said, "McKibben can set all things right. (apologies to
  Alexander Pope)

"Ecology" comes from the Greed oikos logos—laws of (global) housekeeping. A New Yorker article suggested that the current corona virus pandemic could well be seen as a sort of wake-up call to the human race. Gaia (or God or Mother Nature—pick your favorite personification of our one and only home) is sending us a warning that if we don't start treating the planet better, there will be worse to follow. To employ a Genesis metaphor, this is only the first plague and more are in the offing if with our endless pursuit of fun and luxuries we continue our flagrant waste of the Earth's limited natural resources. We can now see that James Lovelock had a point with his Gaia theory (named for an ancient Greek earth goddess), which viewed the planet as a highly complex organism. And like our individual organisms, which have natural immune systems capable of eliminating many threats to our continued well-being, it is

---

76. John Tarrabant, "Quick! What Is Your Original Face?, *Shambhala Sun*, May 2005, p. 77.

capable of eliminating elements that endanger the delicate balance of our ecosystem. Elements like us.

It is worth noting that the word "economics"—which might yet prove to be the name of a false deity whose worship has set its worshipers in conflict with their own chances of survival—is relatively new. It is now defined as the management of material wealth; but Adam Smith, its purported founder in the late 1700s, called it 'moral philosophy' and insisted that whenever market forces worked against the general welfare of the population, it was the responsibility of governments to restore a proper balance of interests. (Compare the Constitution's "to promote the general welfare" with the largely unrestricted pursuit of wealth that marks the current system.)

We might also recall that as children we often threatened offenders with the phrase, "If you do, I'll crown you!" How ironic that the present threat is the 'corona' (crown) virus! According to the Hebrew Bible, the Children of Israel suffered when they failed to heed the prophet's warnings of God's displeasure. We may well take that as an ancient metaphor, but it is clear today that our abuse of nature has real and potentially fatal consequences.

Dame Nature is just now giving us a very uncomfortable "whack upside the head": will we take the warning and change our ways? Or will we again take up our merry path to disaster?

• • •

A definitive dialogue

To: Lloyd Geering
Sent: Sat, Aug 14, 2021 12:46 am
Subject: A non-theist Jesus?

Hi, Lloyd,

Nearing the end of my fifty-page rant on antediluvian theology, it suddenly occurred to me that in view of Lk 17:21 (the Kingdom of God is within/all around you), Mt 13:33 (the sacred and the secular are one), and Mt 5:45 (sun and rain for good and evil alike)—all of which are either red or pink—one might reasonably propose that Jesus was a non-theist. What do you think?

Best,
Tom

To: Tom Hall
Sent: Mon, Aug 16, 2021, 7:08 pm
Subject: Re: A non-theist Jesus?

Hi, Tom,

Jesus was a humanist. He said, "The sun shines alike on the good and the bad."

He was much, much more radical than the developing oral tradition made him out to be.

Note the contrast between Mark and John.

Best wishes,
Lloyd

• • •

Introduction to "A Call for Commitment," a presentation to the New Zealand Sea of Faith Annual Conference 2018—Theme: "Religion for a Sustainable Future."

How the religion of Jesus became a religion about Jesus:

> . . . if you confess with your lips that Jesus is Lord
> and believe in your heart that God raised him from the dead,
> you will be saved. Rom 10:9

"Once Adam is no longer seen as an historical figure, the whole drama of salvation described by Paul in his letter to the Romans is undermined, and the whole soteriological edifice collapses . . . Salvation History, Christ as redeemer and saviour, and the church as the instrument of salvation. We are left with Jesus as the counter-prophet of a radical way of life, and with the personal challenge of his ethical idealism."—Dominic Kirkham

To be part of a sustainable future, Christianity must change from a religion of belief to one of commitment, one that enlarges our vision of reality and thus possesses survival value. We have too long treated religions as belief systems, and Jesus' message has been trivialized by Paul and Luther, who championed salvation by faith alone—a notion alien to the prophet they claimed to represent. The Greek *pistis/pisteuo* (belief, faith, believe) is better rendered "trust" or "faithfulness"; but even these terms name states of mind rather than ethical response, and today we live in a time when not only our religious traditions but our very survival face grave challenges. Any realistic hope for a sustainable religious or ecological future demands an active commitment to *tikkum olam*—repairing the world.

• • •

Conclusion of "A Call for Commitment"

When the dualistic and supernatural elements of classical Christianity that drove many away are rejected or taken metaphorically . . . we may begin to think and act our way into the perilous times ahead.

Although the problems confronting the first-century Galilean peasantry were very different from the existential threats we face today, Jesus' core teachings remain as valid as ever. And like his message, that of a hymn penned to protest the 1845 US war against Mexico has striking relevance. It begins, "Once to every man and nation comes the moment to decide . . ." and goes on to remind us that "New occasions teach new duties / Time makes ancient good uncouth." Today that first line might end, "Do we make LIFE our commitment or commit mass suicide?"

Or if your musical tastes lean more to the popular genre, think of the prescience of these lyrics:

> There'll be a change in the weather, a change in the sea,
> From now on there'll be a change in me;
> My walk will be different, my talk and my name,
> Nothin' about me's gonna be the same.
> I'm gonna change my way of livin', and if that ain't enough,
> I'll even change the way I strut my stuff . . .

Thomas Berry has wisely proposed that true religion is ". . . to live together graciously on this beautiful blue planet . . . and to pass it on to our children with the understanding that the great community of life can nourish, guide, and heal them as it has us."

Or if you like alliteration, let this be your description of religion for a sustainable future: Congregations committed to communal concerns and continued Caretaking of creation here in this critically crowded corner of the cosmos.

Liturgical Items
Calls to Worship

In songs of love and gratitude
We raise our voices here today
Let life and fellowship and food
Come to all humankind, we pray

This lighted lamp is an invitation to worship and prayer.
As the flame burns, shedding light and warmth,
So may a new spirit be kindled in our hearts,
Lighting our ways and warming our lives.

91

Inspire anew our hearts and minds, Great Spirit,
Teach us to craft a prayer so you can hear it;
And lest we try to speak to you in prose,
Remind us still that none among us knows
The who, what, where, or why of your existence.
To help us span the spiritual distance,
Grant us the power of poetry—and of persistence.
Let this grand metaphor inspirit all our labor:
We praise you only as we serve our neighbor.
Help us to act our dream, make real our vision;
And may our noblest hope spur our decision
To reach out to those lost along the way,
To let your love show in our living every day.
Teach us to be poets, teach us how to pray.

A Communion Service

The radical mission of Jesus was to announce the immediacy of God's presence and the accessibility of divine grace to all who sought it.

Central to this vision was the acceptance of all seekers as equals, whatever their nationality, religion, gender, or social standing.

One of the more striking symbols of this shocking proclamation of equality was his habit of eating and drinking with disreputable people. By accepting table fellowship with all, he declared all to be equally the children of his heavenly father.

For many centuries before Jesus' time, the people of Israel had believed that true worship of God required sacrifice—returning to their benevolent but demanding creator a portion of the grain and oil and meat he had provided for them. But even higher in the eyes of both the Law and the prophets, as well as in the teachings of Jesus, was the demand for justice and righteousness. Sacrifice, in Jesus' teaching, involved sharing—in order that the gifts of a just and righteous God might benefit all his children.

It is fitting, therefore, that this ceremony we perform in his memory should be a re-enactment of his last meal with his followers.

Scripture tells us that he took bread, and blessed it, and broke it, and gave it to his disciples as a symbol of his body which he must soon offer in sacrifice.

No one knows just what was said or done at Jesus' last meal with his followers, but the two most likely symbolic messages were these: that all people are welcome at God's table, and that each of us must give generously of himself or herself if the Kingdom/Realm of Righteousness is ever to come to earth.

To these truths we today testify anew.

Prayer—Distribution of Bread—Read Prov. 9:1–16 (below)

"This do in remembrance of me."

Similarly, he took wine, and gave thanks, and offered it in celebration of the truth that God's grace is not to be found so much in Temple sacrifice as in giving oneself to God's service.

Prayer—Distribution of Grape Juice—Read Sir. 24:13–22 (below)

"Drink ye all of it."

Unison recitation of 23rd Psalm

Communion, hymn, benediction, etc. as desired.

Proverbs 9:1–16 (ed.)

Wisdom has built her house,
A solid, seven-pillared structure;
She has laid her table, and furnished it
With the choicest foods and the finest wine.
She has sent her maidens far and wide
To proclaim her invitation to one and all:
"Come to my banquet, you who desire life.
Even the unwise, if they eat my bread, gain understanding,
And the foolish who taste my wine will find enlightenment.
Turn away from ignorance, and follow its descending path no more;
Walk in wisdom's way and live.

Sirach 24:13–22 (ed.)

Thus Lady Wisdom speaks:
"Though sovereign as the tall cedar of Lebanon,
I am yet as a fruitful palm beside the river,
a fine olive tree in the plain,
or a rich vine upon the hillside.
I have spread my graceful branches,
and put forth strong, well-laden shoots;
My blossoms promise a goodly yield,
a harvest of well-being and honor.
Come close, and take your fill of my fruits,
for merely recalling me is sweeter than syrup,
and possessing me more pleasant than honey from the comb.
Whoever feeds on me will hunger still for more;
who drinks my draught will thirst to drink again.
Whoever heeds my teaching will be safe from shame;
who follows my work will never go astray."

Gloria Patri redux (Greatorex)

Fill us, Lord, with your spirit
And help us humbly seek to do your will;
May your ancient call to justice direct the paths we follow;
Teach us with mercy our lives to fulfill.

Amazing Grace redux

This revision of an iconic and widely revered hymn is the result of a long-standing distaste for the antiquated theology represented by the original lyrics. I cannot claim total originality for the text, because it arose from an e-mail correspondence with Dominic Kirkham, an English friend, a highly regarded author, and formerly a Roman Catholic monk and priest for thirty-odd years. The subject, it so happened was "grace"—originally a synonym for gratitude or thanksgiving, a close relative of "eucharist," and thus not so much a gift bestowed as an inward potential for selfless action.

That exchange led to a second stanza prompted by the term "solar ethics," a concept coined by the prolific Don Cupitt, an Anglican vicar, theologian, and philosopher.

The theme of new perspectives evoked for stanza three a motif found in *Reimagining God,* a recent book by Lloyd Geering, the former head of New Zealand's Presbyterian Seminary—namely, the increasingly global and future-oriented nature of any meaningful future theology.

The summarizing fourth stanza could then reflect none other than a first-century Jewish prophet and teacher from Nazareth, whose name and fame are familiar to nearly everyone.

Amazing grace that we might find
In serving others' needs
A glow of hope and peace of mind
Not drawn from ancient creeds.

For when our lives give forth both light
And warmth as does the sun,
An end to mankind's ancient plight
Will have at last begun.

Howe'er we name the Power supreme
That rules the cosmos vast,
'Tis we alone who must redeem
The sins of ages past.

Our lives we therefore dedicate
To those with whom we live:

Not to destroy, but to create;
No more to get, but give.

The Lord's Prayer redux

Eternal Spirit,
Source of all that is and shall be,
Loving Parent in whom we discern heaven,
May the hallowing of your name echo through the universe,
And may your commonwealth of peace and freedom flourish on
    earth
Until all of humankind heed your call to justice and compassion.
May we find the bread that we need for today,
And for the hurts we cause one another
May we be forgiven in the same measure that we forgive.
In times of trial and temptation strengthen us,
From ordeals too great to endure spare us,
And from the power of evil deliver us.
May you reign in the glory of power that is love,
Now and forever.
Amen.

Who are we?

We are a progressive congregation,
seeking an enlightened faith,
committed to an open-minded search for truth,
dedicated to the critical study of Scripture,
an ecumenical view of religious life,
a global and ecological understanding of ethics, and
the promotion of universal faith, hope and love.

Grace for a Church Supper

As the first Christians gathered together to share food and fellow-ship, so we gather here this evening and pray that the same spirit which gave them strength will fill our lives with a measure of its power; and as their hope and trust in your Providence was a beacon that led others to swell their numbers, so may our faith shine that others may in this latter day come to know you.

A Grace for Potluck Meals

At this table we celebrate not one person's self-sacrifice for the salva-tion of many, but the presence of the Divine in everyone; and in sharing food and fellowship we commit ourselves to one another, to the entire human family, and to the indwelling Presence that unites us.

A Grace

Thank you for a gray day etched with bare trees;
We need the starkness to stay in touch with you.
Thanks, too, for a few beech saplings holding fast their bleached
     leaves;
We need to be reminded of the virtue of tenacity.
And thanks for the hopeful pines and firs thrusting green points
     into the drab woods;
We need to be assured that life forever renews itself.
And for the call to re-create our lives with service and joy and grati-
     tude—since we need ever to be born anew—
Our hearty, heartfelt thanks.

Invocation for a graduation ceremony

Great Universal Spirit in whom we live and move and have our being, since you both surround us and live within us, it is perhaps redundant to invoke your presence on this glad occasions; yet in celebrating
this milestone in the intellectual growth of these young men and women
it is only fitting that we should remind ourselves and inform them of the
long upward path that humankind has followed in its quest for the self-
fulfillment that we conceive to be the fulfillment of your purpose for us.

Help us to grow in a wisdom founded upon Aquinas' insight that
your twin gifts of reason and faith can be in conflict only if we lead ourselves astray, and upon Galileo's brave trust that our freedom of inquiry
is the means of your self-revelation.

Help us so to hone our minds that in our search for understanding
we find an ever greater confidence in and reliance upon your infinite
providence. We ask all this in the name of Jesus, the wise rabbi whose
teachings we seek to follow, and whose example we strive to emulate.
Amen.

Verses

A Yuletide Wish (1944)

Candle shining in the night,
Symbol of good Christmas cheer,
Let your gentle, flickering light
Guide us through the coming year.

Crossings

To cross a river
Is to enter a new land, to be reborn.
Joshua was told in no uncertain terms

About proceeding with all due ceremony;
And after the fateful Rubicon,
Caesar would never find things quite the same;
And Benet's John the Son of John dreamed dreams
Upon the mighty Ou-dis-sun's far shore.
And those who sought new promises "Away,
Across the wide Missouri" found instead
New lives in the vast lands that lay beyond,
And a new world they never lived to see
Began to be born.

To cross a street,
To stem the four-wheeled flood and safe achieve
Its farther shore, can be a chancy thing as well;
And as well—for we are blind—may yield
A glimpse of landscapes dimly if at all
Foreseen. Especially if, on the way across,
Someone you thought just happened to be there
Reaches out and gently takes you by the hand
As if to say this portion of the journey
Might be made safer and more pleasant thus –
And suddenly, without a sign, without a sound,
A new world stirs within, and all around.

On first completing Geering's World to Come

Great spirit of the sky and sea and of the earth
Who I know dwells as well in me, and by my birth
Has offered the precious chance to be something of worth,
Give me new eyes to set me free from dross and dearth;
Let glad responsibility teach awe and mirth,
And revel in all humanity.

Humanity

Let me both see my neighbor's need
And not be slow to offer aid
That it may be a selfless deed
And one whose debt is fully paid.

A Christmas Thought (1959)

Into a world grown somewhat gray and cold,
Where warmth and light have become such seldom things
That only by memories are we made bold
To live—or by faith like that of icy springs

Whose crystal cavortings down a bare hillside,
Already in practice for April's glad ballet,
Exult in love that will not be denied—
Into this world grown somewhat cold and gray
An evergreen lifts its tall, tasseled top
To banish from this world the wintery gloom;
And as the world yields up this Christmas crop
Of living green to grace your living room,
So does the timeless Christmas star impart
Its word of grace to shine within your heart.

A Solar Ethic

If you get more than you give,
One brief lifetime shall you live;
But give more than you take away,
And taste eternity today.

A Vertical Paradox

"I am worth as much as you,"
While true,
Yearns upward, much as Eve's son Cain;
And vain
Forever proves such self-promotion.

"You are worth as much as I,"
No lie,
Accepts our common source and fate
To state
As knowledge what must be emotion

In one bound to eternity
Yet free
To take the path of earth each day—
A way
That still avoids the world's commotion.

And ever seeks with downward eyes
The prize
Above all others—as once looked down
Without frown
One tied to a tree in mute devotion.

Zume Lens*
How small and distant
did God seem to be! Then I
reversed my spyglass.

zume is Greek for leaven

Felicity
The little leap of joy I feel
When that pumpkin-colored
Ball of fur vaults into my lap,
Molds himself to its contours,
And eases his head into the crook of my arm
Suggests that they are right who say
We are all family here –
All elements of one fragile web
Spread out across this lovely blue-green ball.

Christmas Questions (1997)
Tell us who this Jesus is,
Speak the message that is his;
Tell us whence he came, and why,
And how he bids us live—and die.

Son of the Galilean sod,
He rose to witness for the God
Who made us all to live as brothers—
Our lives not ours, but one another's.

He came to show the way to life
Amid the world's unceasing strife,
And help us choose, before life's ended,
The means by which it may be mended.

Will we live by Caesar's might?
Or find reward in doing right,
And in our neighbor's joy, delight?

To a Christmas Card Shepherd
Thou silent sentinel
Who watcheth over lambs—
And to whom cometh word
Of a Lamb who, borne in us,

Within our inmost part
If only we will suffer Him
Room in our Inn to be born—
May we too have watchful eyes,
Ears that can hear,
And a firm grasp upon our staff.
O timeless shepherd,
Patient husbandman,
Called to witness
To the springing forth of life
In the bleak winter of the world,
Look, see
In the four rays of that star's light
The rude wood arms that raised
Him in his lowliness high
As Heaven over us;
By thy example
Teach us to keep our eyes alight
Through the long watches of the night
With sentinel sight.

Different Gods (2021)

Surely the Yahweh who ambled in the garden
With our first parents, then drove them out for fear
A second breach might render them his peers
Was not the Elohim who with a word
Called into being heaven and earth and life
Of every kind, and saw that it was good.

Nor was the God who ordered Joshua
To wage a genocidal war on Canaan
That Israel might live secure and free
Cut from the same cloth as Micah's muse,
Whose sole injunction was to lead a life
Of justice, kindness, and humility.

Whatever the creed that drove the heartless Ezra
To cancel priestly marriages and condemn
Mothers and children to shame and desperation,
Its author's deity was not the God
Who inspired the contradicting tale of Ruth,
The alien whose love was holiness.

Could Jonah's mild taskmaster, who exhorted
That prideful prophet to display concern
For all the folk of hated Nineveh
Have led a vengeful post-exilic psalmist
To wish that all the babes of Babylon
Might have their brains bashed out against the rocks?

For Jesus Jews we meet in Didache
And Galilean archivists of Q,
Their Lord was a new David or a sage;
In Mary's Gospel and in that of Thomas
He seems a Spirit with a human form;
Thus early on his nature was in doubt.

And what are we to understand when John's
Report that Jesus (aka "the Word")
Was co-creator of the universe
Beggars belief, only to learn that he
And his father Joseph hail from Nazareth,
A place of generally low repute?

Why is it John has Jesus early on
Declare that to be saved we must ingest
His body and his blood, then near the end,
At that climactic final meal together,
Replaces the salvific loaf and cup
With after-dinner footbaths for The Twelve?

We'll never know why Matthew changed "the poor"
To read "the poor in spirit" and erased
The curses Luke found in their common source,
Nor make good sense of Luke's chronology
That places Jesus in Jerusalem
For six weeks after his ascent to heaven.

When Luke's Paul scolded fellow Jews who failed
To see his Jesus as God's new Messiah,
He prophesied a Gentile supersession:
"They will listen!" But what sort of God
Would on such grounds desert his chosen people
And pave the way that led to Holocaust?

To what broad vision of the great scheme of things
Will you entrust the guidance of the one

And only life you get the chance to live?
From what commitment then derive the strength
To choose and sanctify in word and deed
A way of life that gladdens and fulfills?

A sermon

God's Unemployment Problem
First Unitarian Church, Providence, RI, June 26, 2005)

It requires only a superficial reading of the writings that constitute the Hebrew and Christian Bibles—or, for that matter a passing acquaintance with most secular histories—to recognize that God was once considered to be a very busy fellow. Under one or another of his several names and descriptive titles—God, Yahweh, Elohim, Lord, Adonai, El Shaddai, El Elyon, El Roi, el Olam, Yahweh Sabaoth—he was always and everywhere hard at work. Except for the day of rest he took on that first Sunday. But he appears not to have enjoyed his Sabbath luxury for long, for soon enough he was obliged to turn that noble ban into minutely detailed law, and presumably went to a good deal of trouble enforcing it. And think of all the other functions he was assigned; he—or she, or it—sent or withheld the rain, wind, and storm; regulated the sun, moon, tides, and seasons; carried out his, her, or its divine will by sending kings to war, and often winning their battles for them lest they pridefully take credit for the victory. Also, according to the record, God was quite fond of inflicting women with infertility until in desperation they offered him special prayers. That way the resulting child could be easily recognized as someone very important. On two notable occasions he even pulled off this little trick without being asked—once in the case of a post-menopausal ninety year old named Sarah, and about eighteen centuries later to immortalize an unwed teenager who lived in an obscure Galilean village called Nazareth.

And all the while he had to manage, and sometimes micro-manage, the daily lives and long-term history of millions of people—always, of course, paying primary attention to an unruly, ungrateful , and often rebellious rag-tag bunch of self-impressed Semitic sheep-herders whom he had for some inexplicable reason chosen as his special favorites. Yes, he was very busy!

"Wait a minute," you say—or, I hope you do—"God plays favorites? That's not fair!" You're right. It's not. And that was Job's entirely valid challenge to God. Unfortunately, the author of that story was unable to break out of the theological mold of his times and accept the obvious.

So he "copped out" and made Job knuckle under to a divine bully who had been playing games with him in order to impress Satan. That book came out about 500 BCE, probably during or just after the Babylonian Exile, and may well mark the beginning of God's slide toward the serious unemployment problem he faces today. And a couple of hundred years after Job things got even stickier, when the ancient secular humanist who wrote the book known as Ecclesiastes in effect trashed the whole theological underpinning of the Hebrew Bible and further limited the deity's scope of operations.

But of course, the two of them made only a small dent in human-kind's willingness—indeed our apparently endless desire—to be bought off with nonsense in our search for peace of mind. (In a recent posting, retired Episcopal Bishop John Shelby Spong acutely observed that "Religion is primarily a search for security, and not a search for truth.") Accordingly, just as they were largely deaf to the ethical prophets, the people of Israel, like their Roman oppressors, were not highly impressed by a first-century teacher named Yeshua, the son of that unwed pregnant teenager I mentioned earlier. He tried to inject some common sense into the theological debates of the first century; but within a few years of his untimely but eminently predictable death, he had been sandbagged, dei-fied, and hustled off the stage by an erstwhile persecutor—an unstable, self-intoxicated, religious enthusiast who persuaded people to worship the martyred teacher as a divine savior, and thus rescued them from the hard work of living according to his teaching. For that great favor, the church founded by this super-salesman gave him the title <u>Saint</u> Paul.

Even such spiritual luminaries as Michael Servetus and Giordano Bruno made little impact when they tried to limit the divine resumé; both were burned at the stake for their honesty. The Judeo-Christian tradition had to wait for Galileo to produce hard, scientific evidence before beginning to recognize the terribly unsettling fact that both Bible and Church had long been handing out taffy. It was bad enough that they presented a distorted picture of the world; it was even worse that applying simple logic to the observable facts of life showed that the sup-posedly almighty and all-wise "guy in the sky"—who was also reputed to be an all-loving father and a paragon of justice—was a contradiction in terms. What we had in fact was a sort of Wizard of Heaven, a big voice from behind a carefully constructed screen of pretense. Worst of all, both the voice and the screen were human creations—and not very coherent ones, at that. We had created God in our own confused image. How many important jobs are you going to trust to someone like that? That is if you really think about it. Too bad most folks don't.

Then a couple of hundred years ago, Thomas Jefferson put out an edited version of the gospels, having removed all the passages he considered to be an insult to the intelligence of any reasonably knowledgeable person. He also opined—a bit too optimistically—that with the growth of free public education and general knowledge, it would not be more than a century before all Christians would be Unitarians. Obviously he didn't make much a dent either. But knowledge and reason continued to spread, and you know enough about Darwin's contribution to the erosion of the divine job description, and about Freud's demonstration of our gift for self-deception, to understand why our Father in Heaven began more and more to resemble the Maytag repairman who has less and less to do.

The final blow, of course, has been the growing recognition that heaven and hell, and life after death, and all their related bugaboos are myths that were for centuries used by church and crown to enforce obedience. (Today even the American presidency is often guilty of that antediluvian swindle.) No wonder so many former churchgoers have joined what Jack Spong calls "the church alumni association"—a defection especially evident in Europe where church attendance now runs between six and ten percent of the population. In the minds of many, all that's left for God to do is to play Santa Claus or Dear Abby to people who are in need or in trouble—and who still think that there's something or someone out there somewhere to call on for help, someone who can arrange a special favor if properly ingratiated. When it finally gets through to us that things happen as a result of people's actions and natural laws (including that of chance), all of a sudden God has a lot less traction in human affairs.

No doubt you're aware of most of that, but have you heard about Ludwig Feuerbach and David Freidrich Strauss, eminent Christian theologians who 150 years ago challenged all the supernaturalist hocus-pocus about Christ's divinity and sacrificial death? They focused instead on the life and teachings of Jesus, and discovered that behind the pious myth was a wise and eternally relevant teacher of righteousness. And think about the more than one hundred scholars of the Jesus Seminar who after fifteen years of intense study concluded a few years ago that out of all the various gospel reports of what Jesus said and did, only about eighteen percent are reasonably accurate. And I'll bet only a very few of you are familiar with Lloyd Geering, the Presbyterian minister and scholar from New Zealand who recently wrote *Christianity Without God* and who, along with Jack Spong and a growing number of clergy, insists that the Christian tradition must soon change radically—or die. Consider but three specific proposals: First, the incarnation doctrine must be applied not alone to Jesus, but to everyone, for we are all God's children. Second, the work of atonement (at-one-ment, being one with the universal spirit) is likewise each person's proper quest and responsibility. Third, the real meaning of the resurrection myth is that each believer is daily called to a higher spiritual life and awareness.

Obviously, Unitarian-Universalists are uniquely positioned to be in the forefront of such a reconfiguration of a tradition that they had the good sense to split away from some time ago. And it might prove an invigorating challenge, for to tell you the truth, the UU spiritual diet strikes me as a bit thin. Don't get me wrong; theologically speaking, I'm pretty cholesterol-free. It's just that after fifteen years of preaching from the Bible, I don't think that your favorite place of religious refreshment has a duty to offer nothing stronger than "God-lite." But at least the low-carb regimen doesn't make me gag. A couple of months ago, I attended another church in this area, and by the time the service was halfway over, I could hardly wait to get out in the fresh air again; in fact I had to bail out before they got to the Communion liturgy with its fictitious Last Supper and the exhortation to take a nip and a sip and be saved. My mind felt soiled by all the Trinitarian and mythical baggage that was glibly foisted on the congregation as eternal truth.

So how *could* those who envision a yet more vibrant and progressive religion serve this underemployment of God? Well, we could begin by writing her a new resumé and job description, and maybe we could decide on some realistic new qualifications, and provide an alias or two, and decide what we mean by those new names. Most important of all, I think, God by whatever name should at long last be brought back to earth, thus reversing the process followed by those inspired conjurors who aeons ago projected him into an imaginary heaven. Can that be done? Of course it can! It will take time and effort and repeated and explicit challenges to the incumbent purveyors of fantasy. But if mumbo-jumbo is often enough pointed out for what it is, and if objective accuracy in religious discourse is consistently demanded, then religious literacy and veracity will flourish. Who knows, maybe in *another* hundred years, Mr. Jefferson's dream will have begun to bear fruit. And suppose it should prove to be the case that the G-word represents nothing more than the sum of our highest ideals and noblest aspirations; that would be a pretty good start at redefining what is sacred and helping it to function in our lives. At least it would be honest.

About the Author

Tom Hall, a former English teacher and lay pastor, had the good fortune to join Westar 25 years ago. An Associate Fellow and Life Member, he has edited 70 books and many articles for this group of scholars, to whom he is grateful for a retirement replete with fascinating and productive activity.

CPSIA information can be obtained
at www.ICGtesting.com
Printed in the USA
BVHW040302050122
625486BV00012B/88